PRAISE FOR
THE LAMB'S AGENDA

"Reverend Rodriguez reveals that we are dealing with the clashing of human-interest agendas not far from those my father faced in April 1963. He also proposes the need to go back to the basic founding principles of our nation, which were biblical."

—BERNICE A. KING, FOUNDER AND PRESIDENT, BE A KING ENTERPRISES, LLC (FROM THE FOREWORD)

"*The Lamb's Agenda* is a clarion call for Christians to embrace truth and grace in equal measure. Sam Rodriguez believes that if we can get the balance right, America may be on the cusp of a Third Great Awakening. I pray it will be so!"

—JIM DALY, PRESIDENT, FOCUS ON THE FAMILY (FROM THE FOREWORD)

"*The Lamb's Agenda* is the Christian Manifesto for the church in the twenty-first century and is a must read. The biblical principles presented by Rev. Samuel Rodriguez will revolutionize the church and restore biblical values to a culture that desperately needs renewing. Rev. Rodriguez articulates the relationship between the salvation in Christ and cultural engagement better than anyone. He is a powerful preacher who has skillfully articulated his stirring message of the vertical and horizontal meaning of the Cross into a blueprint for revival and cultural transformation."

—MATHEW STAVER, FOUNDER AND CHAIRMAN, LIBERTY COUNSEL; CHAIRMAN, LIBERTY COUNSEL ACTION; CHAIRMAN, FREEDOM FEDERATION; DEAN AND PROFESSOR OF LAW, LIBERTY UNIVERSITY SCHOOL OF LAW

"Sam Rodriguez is one of the most clear-eyed, clear-headed, articulate, and biblically sensitive younger leaders on the Church's horizon today. His spiritual priorities are righteous, his heart for God and people rise from scriptural values, and his lifestyle of service and practical holiness are verifiably consistent to the Word. He is reasonable and convincing; always keeping his case fixated on Christ, as Lord of the Church. I urge us all toward that humility of heart that will enable us to read, review, and seriously consider *The Lamb's Agenda*."

—JACK W. HAYFORD, FOUNDER
AND CHANCELLOR, THE KING'S
UNIVERSITY–LOS ANGELES

"When you listen to Pastor Samuel Rodriguez's message, you hear a man with a passion to communicate the Message of the Cross and persuade believers to return to the core foundation on which Christianity was established. Samuel is desperate to see the United States of America return to godly values. *The Lamb's Agenda* is a call to action that will impact the reader to reflect on the role the Church must take in these last days. Page after page you will be convicted of the aggressive stand Christians must take in order to establish God's Kingdom on earth."

—REV. ALBERTO M. DELGADO, M.A., TH.D.; SENIOR
PASTOR, ALPHA & OMEGA CHURCH; PRESIDENT,
HISPANIC MINISTERS ASSOCIATION OF GREATER MIAMI

"With the eloquent passion of a preacher, national Hispanic leader Samuel Rodríguez charges all Christians to join personal faith in Jesus with a commitment to social justice—the vertical with the horizontal. This is a clarion call for Christians to impact the public square. *The Lamb's Agenda* will stimulate conversation, even disagreement, but what it seeks ultimately is to generate profound change in the status quo."

—DR. M. DANIEL CARROLL R. (RODAS),
PHD., DISTINGUISHED PROFESSOR OF
OLD TESTAMENT, DENVER SEMINARY

THE
LAMB'S AGENDA

THE LAMB'S AGENDA

WHY JESUS IS
CALLING YOU TO A
LIFE OF RIGHTEOUSNESS
AND JUSTICE

SAMUEL RODRIGUEZ

THOMAS NELSON
Since 1798

NASHVILLE   DALLAS   MEXICO CITY   RIO DE JANEIRO

Published in Nashville, Tennessee, by Thomas Nelson. Thomas Nelson is a registered trademark of Thomas Nelson, Inc.

Thomas Nelson, Inc., titles may be purchased in bulk for educational, business, fund-raising, or sales promotional use. For information, please e-mail SpecialMarkets@ThomasNelson.com.

Library of Congress Cataloging-in-Publication Data

Rodriguez, Samuel, 1969-
  The lamb's agenda : why Jesus is calling you to a life of righteousness and justice / Samuel Rodriguez.
      p. cm.
  Includes bibliographical references and index.
  ISBN 978-1-4002-0449-6
1. Christianity--21st century. I. Title.
  BR121.3.R64 2013
  277.3'083--dc23
                            2012033822

Printed in the United States of America

13 14 15 16 17 RRD 6 5 4 3 2 1

CONTENTS

Foreword
BERNICE A. KING

ON APRIL 16, 2013, WE COMMEMORATE THE fiftieth anniversary of my father's letter from a Birmingham jail. In that letter he responded to a group of clergymen who were chastising his actions for being unwise, untimely, and extreme. The clergymen were looking to appeal to the agenda of man and self-interest while my father's agenda came from above. The spring of 1963 was a dark period for the divided church community. This division was reflective of a broken nation, originally built on biblical principles, which began to lose its discipline and gave into a different agenda. Our nation forgot some of its founding principles and allowed itself to be carried by a slow political machine that only muffled the cries of the people who needed them most.

Reverend Samuel Rodriguez gives us a call to action in this book. He recognizes that the political machine today is repeating its mistakes from fifty years ago. Reverend Rodriguez is reminding us that we have a responsibility to speak up. He is calling on the church to recognize that she is not to compromise her spiritual righteousness in her political activism. Reverend Rodriguez reveals that we are dealing with the clashing of human-interest agendas not far from those my father faced in April 1963. He also proposes the need to go back to the basic founding principles of our nation, which were biblical.

Our founding fathers had the discipline to carry the Bible in one hand and an agenda for democracy in the other. Our history is marked by the efforts of strong leaders like my father, Dr. Martin Luther King, Jr., and my mother, Coretta Scott King. Their tenacity helped carry a nation through upheaval and uprising.

As I reflect, I try to discern what could be the common element possessed by these leaders. The one that stands out is the discipline to stand up for what is right and just. In our zeal for progress and change we have lost our discipline to pursue righteousness and justice. Our lack of discipline puts us in a position that challenges our loyalty to God and His kingdom. Thus, we see the absences of the Spirit of Christ in many arenas of our culture and in the lives of some Christians today.

Have we become a people with two citizenships: a citizen of government and of the Kingdom of God? We are forced to pose this question when we see elected officials compromising themselves to maintain party favor, including compromising their stand for what is righteous and just. We are living in a time that calls for a remnant of people to carry on the Lamb's agenda once again. It is time to guide our country beyond these dark and difficult times.

We need to step back and exercise the spiritual wisdom in this book. We must cast out the dirt of immorality as well as the stones of social injustice being thrown at us. We shall stand firm against the uprisings in our culture. Just as my Latino brother has preached to so many, we in the body of Christ must learn how to meet at the nexus of the cross, where the horizontal and the vertical meet. That nexus he talks about is the blueprint of my father's movement taken from the Sermon on the Mount. That nexus is the basic principle that we learn at the cross: Love.

Hebrews 12:11 says: "For the moment all discipline seems painful rather than pleasant, but later it yields the peaceful fruit of righteousness to those who have been trained by it." We need that call to discipline today so we can bear the fruit of righteousness and love. Reverend Rodriguez describes in chapter 9 how we can do this. He urges us to go back to the basics and become "John the Baptist" leaders. We are to serve with humility, and that needs to take place now.

In the words of my father, it's time-out for paying lip service. Now is the time we must pay with life service. As his daughter, I exhort you to raise the standard and answer this very important question: Where do you place your allegiance? Is it with the donkey, the elephant, or will you exercise the discipline needed to adhere to Reverend Rodriguez's appeal, and take on the Lamb's agenda and advance the Kingdom of God?

Bernice A. King
Founder and President,
Be A King Enterprises, LLC

Foreword

Jim Daly

At Focus on the Family, we often talk about the need for all of us, as Christians, to live lives that are characterized equally by *orthodoxy* and *orthopraxy*. What we mean is that for followers of Christ, right thinking or belief (orthodoxy) must walk hand-in-hand with right actions (orthopraxy). If you place too much emphasis on one to the exclusion of the other, you run the risk of becoming weak and ineffectual in your faith. A heavy emphasis on theology, without practical acts of love and service, rings hollow. But a long list of "good works" can ring hollow, as well, if they are not informed by God's Truth.

We can see this theme echoed throughout Scripture. James warns us that "faith [orthodoxy] without deeds [orthopraxy] is useless" (James 2:20). Paul says that "if I have the gift of prophecy and can fathom all mysteries and all knowledge, and if I have a faith that can move mountains, but have not love, I am nothing" (1 Corinthians 13:2). In God's economy, right thinking and right acting always need to be in proper balance.

"He has showed you, O man, what is good. And what does the Lord require of you? To act justly and to love mercy and to walk humbly with your God" (Micah 6:8). "Religion that God our Father accepts as pure and faultless is this: to look after widows and orphans in their distress and to keep oneself from being polluted by the world" (James 1:27).

My friend, the Rev. Sam Rodriguez, has a deep understanding of this need for symmetry and synthesis between orthodoxy and orthopraxy. In fact, I love the way he uses the cross of Christ as a picture of the perfect balance between the two. The vertical beam, pointing heavenward, orients us toward God Almighty and enables us to know the Truth through Jesus Christ. The horizontal beam causes us to look outward, at the world around us, as that Truth transforms our hearts and compels us to reach out in love to our families, friends, neighbors, and, yes, even our enemies.

On a recent *Focus on the Family* radio broadcast, Sam described this as a "comprehensive biblical worldview where John 3:16 meets Matthew 25." And he has evoked two of the most important preachers of modern times to drive the point home. He challenges us to embrace the humble, evangelistic heart of the Reverend Billy Graham along with the passionate, social justice fervor of the late Reverend Martin Luther King, Jr. I like that juxtaposition! I can see it in Focus on the Family's efforts to highlight the plight of orphans, to protect the lives of preborn children, and to minister to hurting families in Jesus' Name. We certainly don't get the balance right all the time, but we very much see these efforts as part of that comprehensive biblical worldview that Sam challenges us to embrace.

As I read his words, though, I'm reminded of another iconic character: Superman! Although fictional, the Man of Steel also embodies the harmony between truth (orthodoxy) and justice (orthopraxy). However, there is an important distinction to be made here. The comic books tell us that Superman was committed to "Truth, Justice, and the American Way." Sam shares that same passion for truth and justice, but he knows there is only one way: God's way. In fact, "God's way" is really just another take on the title of the book you're now holding—*The Lamb's Agenda*.

As you read the following pages, I hope you'll catch a vision for the personal and cultural transformations that are possible when we embrace the heart of Christ and share it with the world around us. Sam believes that if we can get this balance right—the balance between orthodoxy and orthopraxy, between the vertical and horizontal beams of the cross—America may be on the cusp of a Third Great Awakening. I pray it may be so!

Jim Daly
President,
Focus on the Family

Introduction

THE THIRD GREAT AWAKENING

ENVISION.

Envision a village or town or suburb or city anywhere in North America on a lazy, late Sunday morning in May. Envision, too, the signs of God's simple glories in full bloom, each flower opening to the skies, every blade of grass reaching for the heavens, every child's face turned upward in a smile.

Envision a golf course this Sunday morning, lavish and well tended but with no one on it, a bountiful Walmart with no one in it, a thriving outlet mall with no one hurrying through it.

Envision the bright and shiny new hospital, whose skeleton ER crew treat the occasional bee sting or broken ankle or fainting spell, but who are not at all weary from early Sunday shooting victims or ODs, those sad afflictions of yesteryear, now as obsolete as STDs or HPV or HIV.

Envision the old state prison on the outskirts of town, the concertina wire recycled, the fences pulled down, the cells restructured into classrooms for the new community college where the one-time correctional officers learn altogether different career skills—the local police will not need new officers for years.

Envision Main Street, quiet now on a Sunday morning except for the odd bakery or convenience store, but soon to be bustling with families—the tattoo parlors closed for lack of business, the pawn shops shuttered, the strip clubs faded into memory, the old abortion clinic now a memorial in much the spirit of the Holocaust Museum.

Now envision the real action. You can hear it, sense it, feel the vibration bleeding through the walls of one church after another all over town—in the section that used to be called a ghetto, in the quarter once known as the "barrio," in the community previously gated.

Listen to the pulse from evangelical churches to be sure but also from more established Christian churches and the Catholic churches. Hear it, too, in the old mainline Protestant churches that have shaken out the cobwebs, stopped preaching about yesterday's news, and unapologetically renewed their relationship with Jesus.

Envision aisle after aisle of all these churches filled with children, and every child well dressed and well behaved with a loving mother and father. Envision these intact, prayerful, God-centered families freely sharing their time and treasures with those less fortunate. Envision them, through their generosity, consigning those faceless, family-busting welfare bureaucracies to the history books.

Envision the faces of the people in these churches so lively, so filled with joy in the Lord, so brimming with hope, and so stunningly diverse that phrases like "black church" or "Latino church" or "white church" have lost all cultural meaning.

Envision the spirit of these kingdom culture, Bible-believing

Christians as they reach up to the Lord and reach out to their fellow man, as they sing and pray and praise God without embarrassment, without fear of ridicule, without having to brace themselves for some new battle in a culture war they did not start.

Now, remember the day when these Christian soldiers armed with the Truth and inspired by Christ, gentle as the lamb and roaring like the lion, marched onward and won those battles, not with revenge in mind but reconciliation, not by imposing a religion, but by proposing a relationship. Remember how the Holy Spirit penetrated some very hard hearts, until finally even the most impenetrable skeptics had to concede that life now in the spiritual present was tangibly better than in our materialist past, and emotionally so much richer.

Now celebrate the life made real by the Third Great Awakening, the first in nearly two centuries, and the path God has laid out before us to save this great nation. If we have the character and courage to follow that path, what you are envisioning and celebrating and thanking God for is our very future as a church and as a nation as we follow the Agenda of the Lamb.

"It was the best of times, it was the worst of times," Charles Dickens tells us in the opening of *A Tale of Two Cities*. This much we all have heard before, but it pays to listen to more of the Dickens quote:

> It was the age of wisdom, it was the age of foolishness, it was the epoch of belief, it was the epoch of incredulity, it was the season of Light, it was the season of Darkness, it was the spring of hope, it was the winter of despair, we had everything before us, we had nothing before us, we were all going direct to heaven, we were all going direct the other way.[1]

Dickens was writing in 1859 about an epoch that began in 1775. More than 150 years after Dickens, I feel confident writing these exact words about our present era. Yes, we live in difficult times—times of great uncertainty, consternation, angst, and flux. Yes, secular obituary writers have already begun to pen their half-hearted elegies to American Christianity. Yes, some scholars and leaders within the church have joined that noisy chorus. For reasons of their own, they have come to the unhappy conclusion that Christianity in America will not survive the twenty-first century in any viable or sustainable manner. But have we not heard this all before?

The Roman historian Tacitus, writing nearly two thousand years ago, told us how the Emperor Nero thought he had put an end to that "class hated for their abominations, who are commonly called Christians." Tacitus wrote:

> Mockery of every sort was added to their deaths.
>
> Covered with the skins of beasts, they were torn by dogs and perished, or were nailed to crosses, or were doomed to the flames and burnt, to serve as a nightly illumination, when daylight had expired.[2]

If Christians could survive Nero, if they could survive Lenin and Hitler, then they can survive the materialist present. They have already outlasted the Beatles, whose John Lennon told us nearly fifty years ago: "Christianity will go. It will vanish and shrink. I needn't argue with that; I'm right and I will be proved right. We're more popular than Jesus now; I don't know which will go first—rock and roll or Christianity."[3]

I beg to differ with the premise that the church will vanish and shrink. I seriously beg to differ. I proudly beg to differ. For even though housing markets may crumble, the stock market may plummet, and banks may fail, the church of Jesus Christ is alive and well. Superficially, yes, it is the worst of times, but thanks to Jesus, this is very much the best of times—the season of light, the spring of hope.

Truth be told, I believe the twenty-first century will witness the greatest transformative Christian movement in our history. This movement will affirm biblical orthodoxy, reform the culture, transform our political discourse, and usher in a new Great Awakening. I am convinced, to paraphrase Dickens, we do have everything before us.

This movement, however, will be different from anything we have ever seen. First, it will reconcile the philosophy of Billy Graham with that of Dr. Martin Luther King. Second, it will activate the kingdom culture multiethnic church as the natural home of righteousness and justice. Third, it will serve as the platform for an activist generation, one presently disconnected from the church but seeking to serve a cause greater than itself.

When the time comes, only one phenomenon will drive this Third Great Awakening, and that is the impetus of the cross. I am convinced that God is not done with America and America is not done with God. For at the end of the day our nation will be saved not via the agenda of the Donkey or that of the Elephant. Our nation's only hope is found in the Agenda of the Lamb.

1.

A CROSS MOVEMENT, VERTICAL AND HORIZONTAL

LIFE IS A CROSS. NO OTHER SYMBOL INCORPORATES passion and promise like the cross—a simple symbol depicting two pieces of wood, one vertical and the other horizontal, successfully branded the eternal hope of glory to all mankind.

Madison Avenue and multimillion-dollar campaigns have not been able to reproduce any comparable symbol. The loyalty, commitment, and even, to a great degree, the multigenerational allegiance to a message has been conveyed via the humble conduit of this brand. It is not written on the wood, but instead it is incarnated in the spirit of what it represents—grace and eternal life.

That universal Christian symbol, vociferously and with unbridled persuasion, not only conveys a message of what is to come, but also what life truly is: a cross. Jesus said, "Carry your cross daily and follow me."

The cross is both vertical and horizontal. Vertically, we stand connected to God, his kingdom, eternal life, spiritual truths, divine principles, and glory. Horizontally, to our left and to our right, we exist surrounded by and revealed through community, relationships, family, culture, and society.

Simply stated, the cross is both vertical and horizontal, redemption and relationship, holiness and humility, covenant and community, kingdom and society, righteousness and justice, salvation and transformation, ethos and pathos; it is John 3:16 and Luke 4, orthodoxy and orthopraxy, Billy Graham and Dr. Martin Luther King Jr., faith and public policy, *imago dei* and *habitus Christus*, prayers and activism, sanctification and service, the New Jerusalem and Washington DC.

For too long, people have lived either vertically or horizontally. Few, even in Christian leadership, have succeeded in living, speaking, and ministering from where the vertical and horizontal planes of the cross intersect—the nexus of Christianity, the womb from which the Lamb's agenda flows.

THE NEXUS OF THE CROSS

Historically, white evangelicals have focused primarily on two major issues: life and family. Understandably, black Christians have tended to focus on the social justice elements of the gospel message that speak to issues of poverty, education, and racism. The Agenda of the Lamb reconciles both the vertical and horizontal elements of the cross, a platform of righteousness and justice. In other words, the Christian nexus of a kingdom-culture ethos and a transformational mission directive that is not *either-or* but *both-and*.

This nexus is the place where conviction marries compassion, where the fish intersect with the bread, where truth joins hands with mercy. The next great transformative and prophetic movement in our nation must stand committed to the vertical and horizontal cross, the place where we reconcile the optics of redemption with the metrics of reconciliation.

We need a church committed to saving the lost and transforming our communities, addressing sin while confronting injustice. We need a church that will be pro-life and antipoverty, that will strengthen marriage and end human trafficking. A church is not an either-or proposition; it is a both-and community. It is righteousness *and* justice.

Life is both vertical and horizontal—a cross. The individual can live on one plane or, if a pure nihilist, on no plane at all. But why do either when one can dwell at the strongest point— the center? The balanced soul finds its home at the nexus where faith meets action, righteousness meets justice, and the prophetic intersects with the practical.

A Church-led Movement

These converging conduits of righteousness and justice serve as the platform for the most powerful and catalytic entity on the planet, the church of Jesus Christ. While institutions, nations, governments, and corporations fail, one institution will always live: the church of Christ. Matthew 16:18 says it clearly, "And I tell you that you are Peter, and on this rock I will build my church, and the gates of Hades will not overcome it."

The Agenda of the Lamb can only succeed when the Christ-centered, Bible-believing church leads the way. Why? Never in American history have we experienced long-term sustainable change without the Christ-following community igniting the righteous flame. From the abolitionist movement to the civil rights movement to the pro-life movement, the Christian community has led the way. Christians have always been in the vanguard. Our faith provides the moral imperative. Our God—everyone's God—provides the grace to hear the call and the courage to act. Now more than ever, the Agenda of the Lamb requires the Bible-believing church to rise up once again.

Today, we face at least four major threats to Christianity in America:

moral relativism,
cultural decadence,
spiritual apathy, and
ecclesiastical indifference (the reigning spirit of the
     lukewarm church).

Of all these threats, none is more subversive than an indifferent congregation in a lukewarm church.

THE LUKEWARM CHURCH

Why does a lukewarm church pose the greatest danger to the Christian narrative in our lifetime? Simply stated, a lukewarm, sin-tolerant church lacks the moral authority to speak truth to power. It gives only the illusion of being a spiritual force in a material world. As such, it can be—and often is—co-opted by the forces of evil.

Dietrich Bonhoeffer experienced this firsthand.[1] As a dynamic, Bible-believing Christian in 1930's Germany, Bonhoeffer watched in horror as the "official" German Christian

Church cozied up to the National Socialists then in power. As such, that church gave German Christians the illusion that they could be both good Nazis and good Christians. Many fell under Hitler's sway and politely averted their gaze as he proceeded to move from one evil to another.

Bonhoeffer, however, understood the Agenda of the Lamb and the symbolism of the cross. He knew that only through the grace of God and the power of his Word could he find the strength to insist on social justice for his persecuted fellow citizens, many of whom were not even Christians. He understood that the cross's horizontal plane did not stop at the walls of his church.

As Paul argued in Romans 12:18, "If it is possible, as far as it depends on you, live at peace with everyone." And as Jesus himself commanded his apostles, "Therefore go and make disciples of all nations, baptizing them in the name of the Father and of the Son and of the Holy Spirit, and teaching them to obey everything I have commanded you. And surely I am with you always, to the very end of the age" (Matthew 28:19–20).

This was a radical Christian notion, that all of us, regardless of where we live or what we look like, are brothers and sisters in Christ. This is a notion that Bonhoeffer took seriously. For his efforts, as he always knew could happen, Bonhoeffer was imprisoned and executed. He died a saintly death. Many of his fellow Christians died under Hitler's power as well, but too many of them died loathing themselves for their complicity in their own demise.

None of Bonhoeffer's colleagues expressed his regret more poignantly than Lutheran pastor Friedrich Niemöller. In the beginning of Hitler's rise, he frustrated Bonhoeffer with his lukewarmness, his eagerness to be both a good Christian and a good Nazi. To his credit, Niemöller saw the error of his ways. His resistance to Hitler caused him to be imprisoned for eight years, barely escaping execution. About his path to prison Niemöller famously said:

> When Hitler attacked the Jews I was not a Jew, therefore I was not concerned. And when Hitler attacked the Catholics, I was not a Catholic, and therefore, I was not concerned. And when Hitler attacked the unions and the industrialists, I was not a member of the unions and I was not concerned. Then Hitler attacked me and the Protestant church—and there was nobody left to be concerned.[2]

Christians in China today face many of the same challenges that Bonhoeffer faced in Germany. The Communists who manage the state tolerate Christian church services in the same way that Hitler once did; that is, within the narrow theological boundaries dictated by the State Administration for Religious Affairs. The Christians who heed the words of Jesus Christ unfiltered by the state face persecution.

Among the more prominent of the resisters is the Shouwang Church. The church first started as a family Bible study group in 1993 and expanded to more than ten fellowships by 2005. In growing so quickly, the Shouwang Church caught the eye of the authorities. They "asked" church leaders to join the so-called "Three-Self Patriotic Movement Church," a state-sanctioned brand of Christianity. When church leaders declined the offer, persecution began in earnest.

Authorities prevented church members from meeting indoors. When they began meeting outdoors, authorities discouraged attendance by having congregants arrested, fired from their jobs, beaten, expelled from their respective cities, imprisoned, and "re-educated."[3] Meanwhile, the lukewarm Chinese Christians attended their own church services and watched the ongoing persecution with eyes downcast and mouths shut. Worse, as in Nazi Germany, "Christian" acquiescence allowed the state to boast to the rest of the world of its religious tolerance.

The United States is not Nazi Germany, nor Communist China, but we may be headed down the same spiritual path. Our lukewarm Christians ignored the abolitionist movement when they weren't denouncing it. They pretended not to see the civil rights movement and could not even understand the need for one. As to the pro-life movement, they have worked to subvert its influence. When religious freedom has been threatened, they encouraged the oppressors through their silence or active complicity.

Cardinal George of Chicago in 2010 said, "I expect to die in bed, my successor will die in prison, and his successor will die a martyr in the public square."[4] In 2012, when the Obama administration mandated that religious organizations and others cover the cost of contraception, sterilization, and abortion-inducing drugs in their insurance plans, the Cardinal's pessimism suddenly seemed warranted.

Happily for the administration, there were lukewarm Christians aplenty who found ways to accommodate their beliefs to the dictates of the state. John Wesley, one of the leaders of the first Great Awakening, said, "What one generation tolerates, the next generation will embrace."[5]

Many of the impositions of the state and the culture are less obvious than the contraception mandates. With the intimidating help of groups like the American Civil Liberties Union (ACLU), local authorities have been whittling away at the rights of Bible-believing Christians for the last century. They have been particularly successful in turning public schools into secular reeducation centers. Here, students are force-fed a godless, sex-drenched, materialistic diet on a daily basis, and if they or their parents protest, they are routinely held up to ridicule.

Consider, for instance, the case of Roger DeHart. A high school biology teacher, DeHart spent fourteen years at Burlington High School in Washington State. Each class would spend two weeks studying human origins. Nine days were devoted to orthodox Darwinism, and for one day of those two weeks, DeHart would introduce the subject of intelligent design, ID for short. ID scientists simply argue that there is a larger intelligence shaping the universe and life on earth, and they look for tangible evidence of this.

DeHart would ask students to write position papers stating the best evidences for or against Darwinian evolution, and volunteers would then debate the topic in front of the class. "Overwhelmingly," said DeHart, "these students saw that as the favorite part of biology."[6]

Understand here that DeHart was not taking sides in the debate. He was not arguing for biblical creationism. He was simply allowing his students to poke holes in the Darwinian thesis that all life began and evolved strictly by chance, an argument for which there is precious little evidence.

Ten years went by without complaint, and then one student took his gripe not to DeHart or his principal but to the ACLU. At first, the superintendent and school board gave DeHart their 100 percent backing. When a new superintendent was hired, however, he told the board members that they would be held personally responsible when the ACLU launched a lawsuit in its relentless effort to drive even the hint of God out of the classroom. The board started to buckle.

DeHart made adjustments. He would allow the students to see critiques of Darwinism only by noted Darwinists, not by ID proponents. Even these were rejected. Any supplemental articles DeHart wanted to teach beyond the textbook had to be reviewed by the biologists at the University of Washington. In addition, he had to submit a handwritten summary of all that he was to say in the two-week unit. In the end, he was reassigned to Earth Science. End of controversy. The district hired a PE teacher with no biology experience to take his place. DeHart now teaches at a Christian high school.

DeHart's case is unusual only in that he offered an alternative to the systematic indoctrination students typically receive. That indoctrination is thorough. William Provine, the Tisch Distinguished University Professor of Biology at Cornell University, is one of the few Darwinists honest enough to explain what he and his colleagues are teaching:

> My observation is that the great majority of modern evolutionary biologists now are atheists or something very close to that. Yet prominent atheistic or agnostic scientists publicly deny that there is any conflict between science and religion. Rather than simple intellectual dishonesty, this position is pragmatic. In the United States, elected members of Congress all proclaim to be religious; many scientists believe that funding for science might suffer if the atheistic implications of modern science were widely understood.[7]

What are those implications? "Modern Science directly implies that the world is organized strictly in accordance with deterministic principles or chance," wrote Provine. "There are no purposive principles whatsoever in nature. There are no gods and no designing forces that are rationally detectable. The frequently made assertion that modern biology and the assumptions of the Judaeo-Christian tradition are fully compatible is false."[8]

Lukewarm Christians survive by blinding themselves to what the culture is saying. They always have. In 2006, for instance, the General Convention of the Episcopal Church affirmed, via Resolution A129, that God is creator and added that "the theory of evolution provides a fruitful and unifying scientific explanation for the emergence of life on earth, that many theological interpretations of origins can readily embrace an evolutionary outlook, and that an acceptance of evolution is entirely compatible with an authentic and living Christian faith."

What the Episcopalian hierarchy missed is that five years earlier Roger DeHart lost his job in a public high school for merely suggesting the possibility of a larger intelligence. He never even used the word *creator*. What the children of these Episcopalians are learning in class is what Provine and others are teaching, namely that "there are no gods and no designing forces that are rationally detectable." Evolutionary biology as taught is not "entirely compatible" with a God-centered universe, let alone Christianity. How could it be?

Lukewarm churches condemn themselves to irrelevance by trying to accommodate themselves to evil, whether it be the evil of slavery, of Nazism, of godless Communism, or of the atheistic materialism of the biology lab. They are more worried about placating their critics than they are about pleasing Christ. The gradual degradation of the culture happened only because lukewarm churches allowed it to happen.

Spiritual Apathy

The western part of New York is known historically as the "burnt-over" district. People called it that because the fires of evangelicalism swept the region during the Second Great Awakening. Imagine what they might have called Western New York had the lukewarm church prevailed during this period. The "mildly warmed-over district"? Chances are they would not have called it anything. No one would have noticed a spirit worth labeling.

Like cultural relativism and moral decadence, spiritual apathy is what sets in when the fires burn out. The Greeks had a word for this phenomenon. They called it *acedia*, which meant a loss of enthusiasm for the spiritual life. By naming it, the Greeks acknowledged how insidious it could be, how its presence opened the doors for a host of other vices. When *acedia* rules, moral anarchy cannot be far behind. Reinhard Hutter, a professor of Christian theology at Duke Divinity School, has written authoritatively on this subject. He describes *acedia*, or spiritual apathy, as follows:

> It is the very forgoing of friendship with God—which is the fulfillment of the transcendent dignity and calling of the human person—and the embrace of the self-indulgent deception that there never was and never will be friendship with God, that there never was and never will be a transcendent calling and dignity of the human person. Nothing matters much, because the one thing that really matters, God's love and friendship, does not exist and therefore cannot be attained.[9]

In some ways, *acedia* is a worse affront to God than atheism. Atheism at least implies a struggle. Acedia implies surrender.

It is the reigning ethos of many a lukewarm church. The congregants do not trouble themselves to see God's light beaming down the cross's vertical plane. And seeing no light, they radiate no heat along the horizontal plane. No injustices are fought. No troubled spirits are consoled. No souls are saved. *Church* means little more than an excuse to get out of the house, see friends, and go to brunch afterward.

MORAL RELATIVISM

As Christians, we are uniquely blessed with the light of truth, and it guides our every step. The apostle Thomas expressed concern about the collective mission. "Lord," he said to Jesus, "we don't know where you are going, so how can we know the way?" Jesus answered, "I am the way and the truth and the life. No one comes to the Father except through me" (John 14: 5–6).

For thousands of years before Jesus and for two thousand years since, those who do not know Christ have been struggling to find some firm understanding of truth, some way of delineating between right and wrong. The deeply Christian Dante Alighieri, writing his celebrated *Divine Comedy* about AD 1300, had kind words for those pre-Christians like Aristotle, Plato, Socrates, Democritus, Zeno, Empedocles, Anaxagoras, Thales, Heraclitus, and Diogenes who struggled to discern the truth. We can applaud their effort.

Less understandable are the intellectuals of the last few hundred years who have been exposed to Jesus, rejected his truth, and set out on their own to establish a superior system. They, of course, ignore the Lord God's warning to Adam and Eve, "You are free to eat from any tree in the garden; but you must not eat from the tree of the knowledge of good and evil, for when you eat from it you will certainly die" (Genesis 2:16–17). This was not the Lord's way of insisting that people remain ignorant. It was his way of insisting that they remain humble. Every effort to replace Christianity with a "superior" system of good and evil has failed, sometimes grotesquely.

Those who would replace Christian truth usually do so by insisting that there is no such thing as truth. In school and in the media, kids hear this on a daily basis: what you think is as good as what anyone else thinks; everyone is entitled to his or her own opinion; do your own thing; do what feels good; do what feels natural.

At our universities, students are learning in comparative religion classes that Christianity is no better or worse than Islam or Buddhism. In political science classes they are learning that democracy is no better or worse than Communism, godless or otherwise. In sociology classes—and just about everywhere they turn—students are learning that marriage between a man and woman is no better or worse than other alternatives.

The sayings of our relativist friends often find their way to bumper stickers. One of their overriding goals is to shake the believer out of any strong convictions he or she might have. Some real-life samples:

God wants spiritual fruits not religious nuts
I support the separation of Church and Hate
In the beginning God created the Big Bang
I believe evolution is one of God's creations
Pro-life does not end at birth
Would Jesus be a homophobe?
The Christian Right is often neither

Focus on your own family
Jesus disliked the righteous this time too
Tax cuts for billionaires / What would Jesus do?

Unfortunately, our young people are learning bumper sticker philosophy in their classrooms. The summary of the message is that Bible-believing Christians are nuts, hypocrites, haters, homophobes, busybodies, flat-earthers. To hold strong convictions is to be closed-minded. By contrast, the open-minded have no strong convictions beyond whatever is trending in fashionable circles, and who does not want to be open-minded?

Given the freedom possible in America, we are encouraged to follow where that open mind leads us. "If a man does not keep pace with his companions," said Henry David Thoreau nearly two hundred years ago, "perhaps it is because he hears the beat of a different drummer. Let him step to the music he hears, however measured or far away."[10] People like Thoreau had a great influence on the counter-culture movement of the 1960s, which in turn influenced the people who run our government and media today.

Linda Ronstadt, for instance, put Thoreau's words to music in the song "Different Drum." She shared with her lover in the song the counterculture mantra, telling him she was not ready for "any person, place, or thing" that would "try and pull the reins in on me."[11] Rock star Jimi Hendrix expressed a similar thought even more forcefully, "I'm the one who's gonna die when it's time for me to die, so let me live my life the way I want."[12] Even Frank Sinatra insisted that he would "say the things he truly feels/ And not the words of one who kneels."

In short, he would live his life "my way."[13] (Of note, the deeply, if erratically, Christian Elvis Presley changed the "one who kneels" lyric in his version of the song.)

No one captured the empty ethos of that era more completely

or more destructively than Beatle John Lennon, "I'm not claiming divinity," he once said, although he often flirted with the claim. "I've never claimed purity of soul. I've never claimed to have the answers to life. I only put out songs and answer questions as honestly as I can. . . . But I still believe in peace, love and understanding."[14] For Lennon, that was truth enough. As to Jesus, he "was all right, but his disciples were thick and ordinary. It's them twisting it that ruins it for me."[15]

I could cite a thousand more examples of the same, but rock stars have a way of influencing the culture that cannot be denied. Ronstadt, for instance, had an open relationship with then—and current—California governor Jerry Brown. President Barack Obama has cited Jimi Hendrix's lyrics on more than occasion. And then President Jimmy Carter eulogized John Lennon on his death, acknowledging that he "helped create the mood and the music of the time."[16] The beat goes on.

CULTURAL DECADENCE

It would be easy to write a book on cultural decadence. Many have. Today, however, the problems are so transparent they hardly need further documentation, but one major threat that kids face today, especially boys, is something men of my generation never experienced: the relentlessly destructive flow of Internet pornography.

A tragic side effect of this exposure is that ordinary young men are losing interest in ordinary young women. Many of them are no longer looking for girls who would be good wives and mothers. They are looking for girls who would be good performers, real or otherwise.

What they do need is resistance, response, action. The most

corrupting of these media have found their way to the most vulnerable of our young people, especially those in our inner cities who absorb messages of hate, of violence, of sexual debasement as a matter of course.

To combat this plague, we must absorb the grace that flows down the vertical plane of the cross and channel it left and right. We must take Christ's message of love and hope to those people and those communities who need it most, not just the consumers of this material, but the producers. We must brave the insults that will come our way for being kingdom culture Christians in an environment scarcely more tolerant than that of Imperial Rome.

If we don't take action, we can be confident the lukewarm Christians and the relativists of whatever stripe certainly will not. To fight for something, you have to believe in something first.

Christians carry the antidote to moral relativism, spiritual apathy, and cultural decadence. The antidote is nothing less than the Lamb's Agenda. This cross-contextualized, church-led movement will only succeed if Christ is reintroduced in America as the Son of the Living God. Let a generation arise committed to following the teachings of Matthew, Mark, Luke, and John. Let a generation arise following the precepts of prophetic Christianity rather than popular culture. Let a generation arise ignited by the words in the classic hymn:

> *My hope is built on nothing less*
> *Than Jesus' blood and righteousness.*
> *I dare not trust the sweetest frame,*
> *But wholly trust in Jesus' Name.*
> *On Christ the solid Rock I stand,*
> *All other ground is sinking sand;*

All other ground is sinking sand.
When darkness seems to hide His face,
I rest on His unchanging grace.
In every high and stormy gale,
My anchor holds within the veil.
On Christ the solid Rock I stand,
All other ground is sinking sand;
All other ground is sinking sand.[17]

2.
Prophetic vs. Pathetic Movements

There's a fine line between the prophetic and the pathetic. The *prophetic* is a forward-looking application of truth to power. The *pathetic* meanwhile focuses on the pitiable state of the here and now. The great question facing civic, religious, and academic leaders today is this: What does our nation need in the midst of these pathetic times? There are many potential answers: we need economic renewal; we need to build a firewall against moral relativism and apathy; we must strengthen the family; stand for life; eliminate abject poverty; defend religious liberty; protect God's creation, and much more.

Yet the prophetic antidote to our pathetic reality is not another bailout, stimulus package, or a new political movement. What we need above all is a fresh outpouring of God's Holy Spirit. What we need is a prophetic movement with a socio-political impact rather than a political movement with spiritual threads. There is a big difference between the two. Simply stated, prophetic activism is measured by action. Political expediency is measured by rhetoric. It's time for more action and less rhetoric.

SPIRIT EMPOWERED

Forget Harry Potter and Hogwarts. There are real spirits in the world today. To this day, we often use biblical allusions to capture the essence of these spirits. The spirit of the Pharaoh, for instance, still lives, holding people captive in the Egypt of bondage and fear. The spirit of Goliath, like that of other seemingly unconquerable forces, mocks and intimidates the children of God.

The spirit of Jezebel weakens the knees of men and women vulnerable to perversion and sexual manipulation. The spirit of Absalom divides homes, churches, and relationships, while the spirit of Herod murders infant dreams through abortion, sex trafficking, and extreme poverty.

Yet I have news for you. There is a Spirit that's more powerful than all these spirits combined. The most powerful Spirit alive today is not that of Pharaoh, Saul, Absalom, Goliath, Jezebel, or Herod. The most powerful Spirit on the planet is the Holy Spirit of Almighty God, the Spirit of the Lamb. "'Not by might nor by power, but by my Spirit,' says the LORD Almighty" (Zechariah 4:6).

So to every narrative and spirit that facilitates the platform of moral relativism, spiritual apathy, cultural decadence, and ecclesiastical indifference we say the following: For every Pharaoh there must be a Moses. For every Goliath there must be a David. For every Nebuchadnezzar there must be a Daniel, for every Jezebel there must be an Elijah. For every Herod there is a Jesus. And for every devil that rises up against you there is a mightier God that rises up for you! Hallelujah!

ADVOCATING FREEDOM

"Now the Lord is the Spirit, and where the Spirit of the Lord is, there is freedom" (2 Corinthians 3:17). We live in a world where people find themselves bound—bound by pornography, sexual compulsion, alcohol, depression, loneliness, dismay, anxiety, fear, confusion, the past, failure, defeat—bound by sin.

Why is there so much bondage? It is the enemy's way of constraining us. Jesus said, "Very truly I tell you, everyone who sins is a slave to sin" (John 8:34). The enemy understands that the most dangerous human on the planet is not the one with riches or armies or fame. The most powerful human on the planet is a person set free by the blood of the Lamb.

Why? The reason is simple enough. It was a free man who approached Pharaoh in Egypt and said, "Let my people go."[1] It was a free man who stepped into the promised land and declared, "As for me and my house, we shall serve the LORD."[2] It was a free man who stared down a giant named Goliath and said, "You come against me with a sword, a spear and a javelin, but I come against you in the Name of the Lord God Almighty."[3] It was free young people who refused to bow and showed the power of their will even in the midst of a fiery furnace.[4]

In more recent history, it was free individuals who declared, "We hold these truths to be self-evident, that all men are created equal, that they are endowed by their Creator with certain unalienable rights, that among these are life, liberty, and the pursuit of happiness."[5]

It was a free man who confronted the evil of slavery and then declared after a brutal war:

> With malice toward none, with charity for all, with firmness in the right as God gives us to see the right, let us strive on to finish the work we are in, to bind up the nation's wounds, to care for him who shall have borne the battle and for his widow and his orphan, to do all which may achieve and cherish a just and lasting peace among ourselves and with all nations.[6]

It was a free young man who had a dream that his "four little children will one day live in a nation where they will not be judged by the color of their skin but by the content of their character."[7]

It was a free man who helped "tear down that wall" as he stood driven by his own declaration, "I'm convinced more than ever that man finds liberation only when he binds himself to God and commits himself to his fellow man."[8]

But the greatest expression of a freedom came two thousand years ago when hanging on a tree by his sacrifice, Christ—a free man, freedom incarnate—personified what he declared in John 8:36, "if the Son sets you free, you will be *free indeed*"!

Our freedom stems not from the political preferences of ideologues in Washington DC. Our freedom does not come from the Republicans or Democrats, from the Donkey or the Elephant. Our freedom comes from the Lamb who is on the throne, to whom angels cry, "Holy, Holy, Holy."[9]

Our founding fathers understood this. They uniquely wrote the Declaration that established the nation's relation to God: "We hold these truths to be self-evident, that all men are created equal, that they are endowed by their Creator with certain unalienable Rights, that among these are Life, Liberty and the pursuit of Happiness."[10] Yes, it is the "Creator" who endows men and women with these rights—not the mayor, not the governor, not the president.

The founding fathers subsequently wrote the Constitution that prevented the government from denying us the unalienable rights with which we had been endowed. It was no accident that the very first sentence in the First Amendment of the Bill of Rights declared God's law above man's interference: "Congress shall make no law respecting an establishment of religion, or prohibiting the free exercise thereof."

Similarly, Abraham Lincoln acknowledged that it was God who gives us the right "to see the right." Martin Luther King was even more explicit in his justly famed "I Have a Dream" speech. He concluded with the words of an old African American spiritual, "Free at last! Free at last! Thank God Almighty, we are free at last!" Freedom, he understood, came from God. Man could not grant it. Man could only take it away. The truth that God is the source of our freedom is the same truth, as promised in John 8:32, that we shall know and shall set us free.

Too many people have forgotten this. Too many people look not to "God Almighty" for liberation but to their political party or their elected officials, as though freedom were an earmark that could be lobbied for distribution. Worse, some use the church as a front for their political activities, perhaps none more seductively or destructively in our time than the "Reverend" James Jones.

A self-declared communist, Jones would write of his Christian conversion. "I decided, how can I demonstrate my Marxism," he recounted years later. "The thought was 'infiltrate the church."'[11] In time, he would pervert the words of Martin Luther King and substitute the anti-prayer, "Free at last, free at last. Thank socialism almighty we will be free at last." As history recorded, he "freed" his followers to mass death at a place called "Jonestown" in the jungles of South America. And before you laugh at a "Kool-Aid" reference, remember that three-year-olds don't commit suicide.

Jones was following a well-trodden path. In the 1920s and 1930s, some Marxist intellectuals began to see that the workers of the world were not about to rise up and overthrow their capitalist bosses without some serious help from their presumed betters. Social philosophers like Antonio Gramsci in Italy and Max Horkheimer in Germany began to hammer out an alternative approach to Marxist revolution often referred to as "critical theory."

These cultural Marxists saw religion as the critical infrastructure that made Western civilization work, not just for the middle classes but for the working classes as well. Generally speaking, they were of the opinion that if religion could be co-opted and turned against itself, it could be used to pull down the culture and the economy. The trick was to convince religious leaders to shift their emphasis from Jesus on the cross to man in all his daily misery.

If thoroughly propagandized by the media and intellectual elite, pastors would focus on the here and now, not the hereafter. They would energize their followers not to seek salvation but to demand economic justice. They would evangelize not to save souls but to subvert the economic order, and in doing so all the media hosannas would be theirs. It is worth noting that the *Los Angeles Herald* named James Jones the "humanitarian of the year"—the year before he led nearly one thousand people to their deaths.

"This revolution also presupposes the formation of a new set of standards," said Gramsci, "a new psychology, new ways of feeling, thinking and living that must be specific to the working class, that must be created by it."[12] This new morality had no place in it for Jesus Christ. Unfortunately, far too many faith leaders, many of them well meaning, fell for this phony liberation.

It is well past time for a generation to rise up and articulate the true message of freedom, to tell the world that through Christ, the individual can be free from sin, free from fear, and free from condemnation. It is past time for believers to lead a movement communicating the true message of freedom. It's time to tell the world that through Christ, the individual can be free from that ultimate anxiety, eternal darkness. As Paul said to the Romans, "There is therefore now no condemnation to them which are in Christ Jesus, who walk not after the flesh, but after the Spirit" (Romans 8:1 KJV).

THE TEA PARTY: PROPHETIC OR PATHETIC?

Today, we bear witness to political movements from Occupy Wall Street to the Tea Party. These movements differ significantly in demands but share, at least in their collective presentation, an indifference to the compassionate message of the gospel.

We understand what political activists may not, namely that the antidote to moral relativism, cultural decadence, spiritual apathy, and ecclesiastical indifference is to be found in the teachings of Jesus Christ. Those teachings can be disseminated widely only through a Third Great Awakening. As history tells us, the first Great Awakening swept America, and much of Western Europe, in the 1730s and 1740s. At the time, the established

churches had begun to grow lukewarm. Led by ardent Christians
like the Wesley brothers and George Whitefield, this new spiritual renewal began in England and soon found its way to the
colonies. The renewal awakened literally hundreds of thousands
of Americans, most of them already churched, to the power
of prayer and genuine intimacy with Christ. Importantly, the
Awakening also reached out to women and to African Americans
and sowed the seeds of a greater freedom within them.

As Whitefield said—and at the time it was a radical thing to
say—"For in Jesus Christ there is neither male nor female, bond
nor free; even you may be the children of God, if you believe in
Jesus."[13]

Like Whitefield, John Wesley saw the movement of the cross
on both planes, vertical and horizontal. "Do all the good you can,"
he said. "By all the means you can. In all the ways you can. In all
the places you can. At all the times you can. To all the people you
can. As long as ever you can."[14] Wesley cautioned his followers,
however, not to lose sight of their inspiration to do good:

> In using all means, seek God alone. In and through every
> outward thing, look only to the power of His Spirit, and the
> merits of His Son. Beware you do not get stuck in the work
> itself; if you do, it is all lost labor. Nothing short of God can
> satisfy your soul. Therefore, fix on Him in all, through all,
> and above all.[15]

By inspiring the colonists to confront complacent and occasionally corrupt ecclesiastical authorities, the Great Awakening
had the effect of showing them they had the power to confront
corrupt civil authorities as well. They came to see that real freedom flowed from God, not from a British king, and a generation

after the Great Awakening, the colonists would courageously and successfully demand that freedom.

In the early nineteenth century, a Second Great Awakening swept America. Even more than the first, the second awakening stimulated Christians and non-Christians alike to move horizontally toward their neighbors, as well, of course, as vertically toward God. The movement spread westward with the population and helped a rugged frontier people embrace a larger, more communal vision than the rough-and-tumble of the here and now.

Just as importantly, this Bible-based movement inspired its participants to launch critical social movements such as abolitionism, temperance, expanded suffrage, prison reform, and communal care of the mentally and physically impaired. Let no one forget where these early reformers drew their courage and their inspiration. On the execution of his colleague John Brown, abolitionist William Lloyd Garrison said:

> God will make it possible for us to form a true, vital, enduring, all-embracing Union, from the Atlantic to the Pacific—one God to be worshipped, one Saviour to be revered, one policy to be carried out—freedom everywhere to all the people, without regard to complexion or race—and the blessing of God resting upon us all! I want to see that glorious day![16]

Both awakenings had a positive and permanent impact on America precisely because they were God-centered. Even after the fervor peaked, many of the changes, both in the faithful and in the larger community, remained because they had a solid foundation. By contrast, the two primary movements of the last few years—the Tea Party and Occupy Wall Street—are built on sand. Although individual participants, especially in the Tea

Party, have a deep faith, faith has not been a part of either collective mission.

The Tea Party functions as a conduit channeling grassroots frustration about the growth of government in terms of size, cost, and intrusiveness. The Americans who participate see Uncle Sam growing while the American dream simultaneously shrinks. Although not controlled by the Republican Party, this anti–big government, anti–higher taxes movement has helped shore up the Republican base.

From its inception until today, however, activists have deferred from addressing any so-called family values or cultural wedge issues, at least under the umbrella of the "Tea Party." This is a strategic decision. It accomplishes two goals. One is that it creates a bigger tent under which to gather participants. The second, ironically, is that it lessens media resistance. To be sure, the mainstream media have no fondness for the movement, but they would have been horrified had the Tea Party been conspicuously faith-based.

That much said, Christians are disproportionately supportive of the Tea Party goals. According to a Pew Research Center survey, white evangelicals agree with Tea Party positions by a greater than 5 to 1 margin. Atheists and agnostics, on the other hand, disapprove of those positions by an identical 5 to 1 margin.[17]

The headlines suggested a generalized media anxiety about Tea Party motives. "The Christian Right in Disguise?" worried the *Daily Beast*.[18] "Tea party: Libertarian revolt or religious right in disguise?" fretted the *Christian Science Monitor*.[19] "Is the Religious Right Taking Over the Tea Party?" asked a concerned *Huffington Post*.[20]

In fact, however, although formidable in both size and influence as made evident in the 2010 primary elections, the Tea

Party represents the secular wing of the GOP. If the Tea Party movement does find Jesus, or if it collectively experiences a "road to Damascus" moment, then America will see a grassroots movement on steroids. This possibility alarms a media that is disproportionately hostile to the Christian enterprise.

What the media fear, perhaps above all, is that Christians in the black and Hispanic communities will find common cause with their white Christian brethren. If all ethnic groups drew inspiration from the cross's vertical plane and followed the cross's horizontal plane to the heart of the Christian community and beyond, the result would be truly formidable. The media would have genuine cause for concern.

For a variety of reasons, people of color who do adhere to a strong faith narrative and share Tea Party concerns about the size of government seem uncomfortable with the Tea Party. The Tea Party still suffers from the same marketing and demographical dissonance as the Republican party: too male, too old, and too white.

While the Tea Party may significantly shift the Republican party to the right, it has yet to be determined if the nation is willing to follow suit. For the Tea Party to become mainstream it will require faith and family values components and an intentional diversification process. Instead of shifting the Elephant toward the right, a conservative insurgency should focus on shifting the Elephant toward the cross. After all, a party without chips and salsa is not a party at all.

OCCUPY WALL STREET: PROPHETIC OR PATHETIC?

The participants in the "Occupy Wall Street (OWS)" movement across America and the world have almost no overlap with Tea

Party participants. They tend to be considerably younger, less stable, and less likely to be employed. Their goals are also more amorphous and diverse. In general, they seem to be protesting economic inequality, greed, corruption, and corporate power. Their slogan, "We are the 99 percent," suggests that the 1 percent are the problem, that they have somehow swindled the rest of the citizenry out of its fair share.

For reasons that have nothing to do with the reality on the ground and everything to do with the reality in America's newsrooms, OWS has gotten generally better press than the Tea Party. The Tea Party movement, which began more than two years before OWS, was constantly monitored by the media for racism, hate speech, and violence. The media had close to no success finding any of these. The OWS movement has shown ample signs of all the above, but the media have tended to avert their gaze lest they notice.

The movement has a curious relationship with Christianity. Occasionally, anti-Christian sentiment found an outlet as it did in Rome when the Occupy crowd attacked a Catholic church, desecrated a statue of the Virgin Mary, and destroyed a crucifix. In Washington, in January 2012, as many as twenty Occupy types disrupted the thoroughly Christian, first-ever official March for Life Youth Rally. They stood and shouted pro-abortion chants and drowned out the speakers.

Running quietly through the OWS movement is a virulent strain of anti-Semitism as well. It was not hard for inquiring reporters at any major Occupy site to find a protestor willing to share his or her opinion on a perceived Jewish threat. For instance, protester Patricia McAllister from Los Angeles, California, said, "I think that the Zionist Jews, who are running these big banks and our Federal Reserve, which is not run by the federal government . . . they need to be run out of this country."[21]

Even the *New York Times* acknowledged "the flashes of anti-Semitism" at the Wall Street site, but offset that quick report with the "distinctly Jewish flavor" of other encampment activities.[22] To be sure, the mainstream media were reluctant to air anti-Semitic rants, but one could find scores of them through the social media.

Not surprisingly, many priests and ministers in the Christian social justice movement found their way to the various OWS sites. Ironically, if the Tea Party did its best to distance itself from Jesus Christ, the Occupy crowd and its allies often tried to co-opt him. Here are some sample headlines: "Would Jesus Occupy Wall Street?" "Would Jesus Christ Participate in Occupy Wall Street?" "What Would Jesus Do About Occupy Wall Street?"

Even the Vatican found potential common cause with OWS. "The Vatican is not behind any of these movements, but the basic inspirations can be the same," said Cardinal Peter Turkson, president of the Pontifical Council for Justice and Peace. "If people can hold their government to account, why can we not hold other institutions in society to accountability if they are not achieving or not helping us live peacefully or well?"[23]

Personally, I think the good cardinal is being too optimistic. As I noted earlier, the next Great Awakening must center itself at the nexus of the cross, the place where the vertical and horizontal cross meet—the place where we reconcile redemption with reconciliation. From my perspective, though, the Occupy movement ignores the vertical for the horizontal. "The protesters don't talk much about Jesus or God," Lisa Miller wrote thoughtfully in the *Washington Post*. "Nor do they offer explicit guidance on transcendent, higher principles." Miller continued:

If he settled for a while in Zuccotti Park, Jesus might find himself disappointed in the fractious, secular nature of it all. For Jesus, the first thing—the only thing, really—was God. His ministry was an effort to help guide people toward a kind of moral perfection before the coming of the Kingdom of God.[24]

Based exclusively in a raw form of social justice without divine inspiration, the movement elevates envy to the level of virtue, community to the level of divinity. These godless utopian movements—from the French revolution to the Cambodian one—always, always end badly. Bonhoeffer saw this firsthand; when the authorities no longer need to co-opt Christians, they end up killing them.

3.

NOT THE DONKEY, NOT THE ELEPHANT, BUT THE LAMB!

THE KINGDOM OF GOD IS NOT RED STATE OR blue state, liberal or conservative, Democrat or Republican, but righteousness, peace, and joy in the Holy Ghost. The time has come for all Americans of all backgrounds, ethnicities, traditions, and political views to lay aside the often simplistic and divisive rhetoric of blue and red, Elephant and Donkey, conservative and liberal, and embrace the inclusive, all-encompassing, transformative power of the cross in culture, society, politics, and life.

While politicians will either push toward the extremes of liberal or conservative policy or, even worse, toward a muddy and unprincipled middle ground, the Agenda of the Lamb remains the one viable guideline for anyone who wishes to experience a new wave of righteousness, justice, and cultural transformation.

When Abraham took Isaac to be sacrificed, Isaac said, "I see the wood and I see the fire, but where is the lamb?" Abraham at least was looking. Too many players on our nation's stage cannot begin to look because they do not yet know what they are missing. Instead, they seek answers in the one-dimensional ideologies at hand: a cold libertarianism on the right, a godless utopianism on the left. These ideologues are discouraged when they do not prevail and disenchanted when they do. Things never work out as planned.

In fact, political engagement can only result in vertical and horizontal transformation when exercised as an act of prophetic witness. In other words, a citizen's political framework must derive from his or her prophetic optics. Their politics must be an extension of their Christian worldview.

Donkey vs. Lamb

There are many good, Christ-loving, Bible-believing Christians who identify themselves as Democrats. This is particularly true in communities of color. It is not at all hard to find a large number of pro-life, pro-family African Americans and Hispanics who vote Democrat.

Yet herein lies the problem. The Donkey's agenda runs counter in many respects to the Lamb's Agenda. While Democrats attempt to engage the horizontal by expressing concern for the poor, the alienated, and the marginalized, they compromise the process by ignoring the vertical. In other words, they attempt to seek justice without acknowledging the Judge.

Many in the Donkey camp take a hostile position toward the followers of Christ. This has not always been true. Fifty or so years ago, there was no discernible difference in the church-going patterns of Republicans and Democrats. Today there is. According to a recent Gallup poll, Republicans are 50 percent more likely to attend church weekly than are Democrats, and Democrats are twice as likely to express no religious affiliation.[1]

Although the percentage of Americans who go to church regularly has remained largely stable over the last half century, the percentage that do not identify with any religion has grown significantly. A substantial majority of these people are at home on the left side of the political spectrum. Many of them are openly hostile to the Christian enterprise. They look upon Christians as bigoted, homophobic, backward, uneducated, archaic, intolerant zealots who resonate more with our past than with our future as a nation.

In 1993, for instance, without even meaning to insult anyone, a *Washington Post* reporter casually referred to traditional Christians as "largely poor, uneducated and easily led."[2] This slur made it past at least a few editors and onto the front page without anyone noticing just how offensive—and false—the comment was.

Comedian Bill Maher, a major donor to Democratic causes, has made a career of attacking Christians. In his film *Religulous*, Maher offered up this secular jeremiad on religion in general and Christianity in particular:

> The plain fact is, religion must die for mankind to live. The hour is getting very late to be able to indulge in having key decisions made by religious people, by irrationalists, by those who would steer the ship of state not by a compass, but by the equivalent of reading the entrails of a chicken.[3]

If Maher were an exception, he would hardly be worth talking about, but unfortunately his brand of hip nihilism resonates among the young who have not had enough faith formation to know otherwise. "Rational people, anti-religionists, must end their timidity and come out of the closet and assert themselves," Maher urged his audience. "And those who consider themselves only moderately religious really need to look in the mirror and realize that the solace and comfort that religion brings you actually comes at a terrible price."[4]

In 2008, when the election in California featured a proposed amendment to define marriage as a union between a man and a woman, a group of Hollywood celebrities felt comfortable producing a video that lobbied for same-sex marriage and casually libeled Christians in the process.

In the three-minute video, a group of black-clad Christians crashed a hippie beach party with a scheme to "spread some hate and put it in the Constitution." As the hippies and Christians sparred back and forth, "Jesus" entered the scene as played by the comic actor Jack Black. When the Christians raised biblical objections to homosexual acts, Black cut them to the quick. "Leviticus also says shellfish is an abomination," said Black as Jesus. "Bible says a lot of interesting things like you can stone your wife or sell your daughter into slavery."

The actor Neil Patrick Harris then tried to convince the alleged Christians that same-sex marriage is good for the economy in that there is money to be made from gay weddings and divorces. This appeal to mammon worked, and the Christians conceded that they had been "such fools" for daring to insist that marriage should remain, as it has always been, between a man and a woman.[5]

I cite these examples to show how safe our friends on the left feel not just in criticizing the Christian experience, but in defaming it. They would not dare express this kind of bigotry against any other group I can think of with the exception of Mormons.

(Note, for instance, the Broadway laugh riot, *The Book of Mormon.*) Had these Hollywood worthies made a similar video attacking, say, Muslims or Mexican-Americans or homosexuals, their careers would have ended on the spot.

The Donkey's media delivery mechanisms routinely offer up anti-Christian imagery that attempts to persuade the American populace, especially the young, that the Christian community stands against change, embodies intolerance, and poses a danger to the kind of godless utopia various dreamers have conjured. "Imagine there's no heaven,"[6] John Lennon asked his followers. But then again so did Vladimir Ilyich Lenin, and Lenin, unfortunately, delivered.

Christianity, however, is a stubborn foe. After fifty years running of anti-Christian agitprop, some 76 percent of Americans still identify themselves as Christian. Add to this mix the thriving (and multiplying) Hispanic immigrant community, and Christianity will in all probability maintain its dominance. One overlooked fact is that nonbelievers tend to become so focused on their own lifestyles that they cannot be bothered to have children. The demographics of faith are worth a book of their own, but suffice it to say that committed Christians in the United States have at least twice as many children per couple as nonbelievers.

As the prophets of moral relativism approach the podium of secular humanism to transmit the message of a horizontal utopia without a vertical alignment of righteousness and justice, the ideological descendants of the Puritans and Pilgrims within the Donkey's camp must decide to either redeem the narrative or vacate the premises. The problem today is that some Democratic activists see winning the religious vote not as a genuine cause, but as a campaign strategy.

On the other hand, President Obama deserves some credit for reengaging a positive Christian narrative within the public square. From celebrating the resurrection of Jesus Christ at an annual Easter prayer breakfast to continuously referencing biblical passages, President Obama seems to demonstrate and, for that matter, affirm the reality that our nation carries a strong faith ethos that cannot be ignored.

At the National Prayer Breakfast in February 2012, for instance, Obama spoke openly about how his faith influenced his policy. "We can all benefit from turning to our Creator," said the president, "listening to Him." He attributed several of his recent decisions to "the biblical call to care for the least of these—for the poor; for those at the margins of our society."

Interpreting Obama's comments as a strategic realignment to capture the center, pundits on the left chose not to criticize his seemingly overt Christianity. Obama's predecessor, George Bush, had no such luck. When he spontaneously cited "Jesus Christ" as his favorite political philosopher in a 1999 debate, he started a firestorm that raged throughout his presidency. In Googling "George Bush Christian fascist," I get more than eleven million hits and article titles like "George Bush and the Rise of Christian Fascism," "Apocalypse No! Christian Fascism? and the Nazi Legacy," and "Dubya the Christian fascist." Unfortunately, today, in the land of the Donkey, Christianity is acceptable as long as it exists on the margins—tepid and unobtrusive.

President Obama's Prayer Breakfast statement stands juxtaposed to the administration-issued mandate requiring that faith groups provide paid coverage for contraception, sterilization, and abortion-inducing drugs. Such mandates fly in the face of Catholic teachings and that of other faith groups as well. The media, the president's pro-abortion allies, and lukewarm

Christians of all denominations rushed into the breach to assure their audiences that this was not an issue of religious liberty but of basic health care. They may have convinced themselves, but they reminded many Americans that the Donkey still has serious issues with the Lamb.

The Donkey's de facto hostility toward the Lamb became evident months prior to the 2012 presidential election, when President Obama expressed an "evolution" of opinion regarding marriage. While the president expressed to Pastor Rick Warren in 2008 his commitment to marriage as a union between one man and one woman, the 2012 President Obama evolved into supporting same-sex marriage.

Immediately, I issued the following statement that was subsequently included and referenced in articles and presentations by *Fox News, Charisma Magazine,* CNN, *New York Times,* and others:

> First, as Christians we must stand committed to reconciling the vertical *Imago Dei,* the image of God in every human being with the horizontal *habitus Christus,* the habits and actions of Christ. This requires a new narrative, an alternative discourse where we stand for truth without sacrificing civility.
>
> It is within this context that we express our deep disappointment in President Obama's change of position on the vitally important issue of marriage protection. Marriage has always been and should always remain the union of one man and one woman. Even as we stand for traditional marriage, we affirm that the image of God lives in all human beings: black and white, rich and poor, straight and gay, conservative and liberal, citizen and undocumented.

Our challenge is to see the image of God in the suffering, the marginalized, the oppressed, and the hurting. Our challenge is to see the image of God in every human being including those we disagree with. Our challenge is to see the image of God in those that oppose us. Our challenge is to see the image of God even in those that persecute and slander us. Our challenge is to see the image of God in friend and foe, acquaintance and stranger, strong and weak, oppressor and liberator.

We believe this approach is biblical, not political. As followers of Christ, we stand committed to advancing not the agenda of the Donkey or the Elephant but only the Agenda of the Lamb. The agenda of Christ is one of righteousness and justice, sanctification and service, covenant and community, holiness and humility, conviction and compassion. It is this agenda that provides the moral imperative to defend biblical truth with love and civility.

While President Obama's support of same-sex marriage does not reflect the sentiment of either the majority of African Americans or Hispanics and places him at odds with two segments of the electorate that celebrated his election in 2008, we must respond with both civility and conviction.

To Hispanics and African Americans, our support of the biblical definition of marriage is not a matter of politics, but a matter of faith. It is our faith that compels us to care for the poor and speak against injustice. It is our faith that prompts us as evangelicals to speak out against bullying and against the persecution of gays and lesbians in third world countries. It is our Christian faith that requires us to uphold the biblical definition of marriage as a sacred union between one man and one woman.

To our community, supporting the traditional definition of marriage is not about being anti-anyone or anything. We understand that a marriage with mom and dad in the home serves as the primary antidote against teen pregnancy, gang activity, drug abuse, juvenile delinquency, and many social ills.

Hence, the great concern stemming out of the president's declaration is whether or not he will pursue federal public policy initiatives that in essence redefine a sacred institution whose definition stems from natural law consistent with a Judeo-Christian worldview. This is, of course, in addition to the recent HHS mandate that infringes on the first amendment rights of religious organizations.

At the end of day, Bible-believing Christians are both in support of biblical marriage and against homophobia. We desire that all Americans embrace life, enjoy liberty, and pursue happiness, without exception.

Yet, we also desire for our elected officials to pursue policy initiatives that advance the common good, using language that brings us together rather than tears us apart. As the Scripture commands, we will pray for President Obama, for his family and for wisdom as he leads our nation.

We will also pray that the president will defend the religious liberties of Americans who, because of conscience and conviction, do not view this issue via the same lens he recently engaged.

Finally, we pray that his support of gay marriage does not exacerbate the growing intolerance of a Christian worldview, which is wholeheartedly embraced by a majority of the African American and Hispanic communities.

As a result of moves like this, there is a growing dissonance between the Donkey and the Lamb. Statistically, while the Donkey identifies African Americans and Hispanics as members of its base, these two communities continue to thrive in their Christian belief. In other words, unless the Donkey reconciles with the Lamb, the Donkey may finish this century in the pony show of the politically obscure.

ELEPHANT VS. LAMB

The Elephant must overcome a whole series of distinct obstacles if it is to embrace the Agenda of the Lamb. Some are found within the party. Some are found without. Some are found both within and without.

Perhaps no political party anywhere in the world had a more honorable founding than the Republican party. In the decade before the Civil War, it emerged from the side of the Whig party specifically because the Whigs would not move horizontally on the cross and embrace a justice agenda. The outstanding justice issue at that time was, of course, slavery. Although Abraham Lincoln was not a churchgoer and had not fully embraced Jesus Christ, he understood the source of his party's justice mission, as he declared in his second inaugural address a month before war's end in 1865:

> Fondly do we hope—fervently do we pray—that this mighty scourge of war may speedily pass away. Yet, if God wills that it continue, until all the wealth piled by the bond-man's two hundred and fifty years of unrequited toil shall be sunk, and until every drop of blood drawn with the lash, shall be paid by another drawn with the sword, as was said three

thousand years ago, so still it must be said "the judgments of the Lord, are true and righteous altogether."[7]

Following Lincoln's assassination, the so-called "Radical Republicans" in Congress sustained the party's justice mission in its effort to integrate those recently enslaved into society. Ultimately, they did not succeed. To ensure success, the party would have needed a leader as charismatic in every sense as Lincoln. They did not have this in Andrew Johnson. Johnson was, however, a devout Christian, one whose vision of the church's role in the state would ensure that he be branded an extremist today. Johnson said:

> I do believe in Almighty God! And I believe also in the Bible. . . . Let us look forward to the time when we can take the flag of our country and nail it below the Cross, and there let it wave as it waved in the olden times, and let us gather around it and inscribe for our motto: "Liberty and Union, one and inseparable, now and forever," and exclaim, Christ first, our country next![8]

By 1877, twelve years after the war, in the face of relentless opposition both in Congress and in the guerilla-thick woods of the South, the Republicans had exhausted their will and abandoned their mission. One reason for their ultimate failure was that they had failed to convince America that integration was a Christian imperative. From this point on, in both parties, politics was mostly—but not exclusively—about business.

The 1960s brought about a number of changes in party dynamics. Up until then, the Democrats had been the party of segregation and Republicans the party of civil rights. Jackie

Robinson, for instance, was a Republican. The Democrats, however, held the White House and Congress throughout most of that pivotal decade. The Democrats led the charge—with considerable Republican help—to assure African Americans basic rights, and in the process they won the allegiance of the great majority of black voters, an allegiance they have held ever since.

Fifty years ago, Democrats saw the connection between fighting for the rights of the unborn and fighting for the rights of minorities. Consider this compelling argument for life at the 1977 March for Life in Washington:

> There are those who argue that the right to privacy is of [a] higher order than the right to life. . . . That was the premise of slavery. You could not protest the existence or treatment of slaves on the plantation because that was private and therefore outside your right to be concerned. . . . What happens to the mind of a person, and the moral fabric of a nation, that accepts the aborting of the life of a baby without a pang of conscience? What kind of a person and what kind of a society will we have 20 years hence if life can be taken so casually?[9]

The speech was made by none other than Jesse Jackson. Born out of wedlock, Jackson took a personal interest in the issue. "From my perspective," he argued convincingly, "human life is the highest good, the *summum bonum*. Human life itself is the highest human good and God is the supreme good because He is the giver of life."[10]

At roughly the same time as Jackson's speech, Democrats started courting—and eventually captured—the emerging feminist movement. To secure this allegiance, the Democrats nearly abandoned any commitment to life and family issues.

"Wanted or unwanted, I believe that human life, even at its earliest stages, has certain rights which must be recognized—the right to be born, the right to love, the right to grow old," wrote the late Senator Ted Kennedy in 1971. "When history looks back at this era it should recognize this generation as one which cared about human beings enough to halt the practice of war, to provide a decent living for every family, and to fulfill its responsibility to its children from the very moment of conception."[11]

At the time, Kennedy seemed to understand that the protection of life was an extension of the cross's horizontal plane as were other social issues. Ambitious to a fault, he moved on, as did every other ambitious Democrat, including Catholics like himself. By the end of his long senate career, Kennedy was getting a 100 percent score from abortion rights groups.

Meanwhile the Republicans, whose country club element was indifferent, if not hostile, to life issues, moved into the void. Once the dust had settled, the Republicans held the allegiance of most Bible-believing Christians, but much of the Republican old guard remained leery of those Christians and their "family values," a term that the Republican elite mocked almost as much as the media and Democrats did. To stake their vertical position on the cross, religious conservatives inevitably faced opposition from the so-called "fiscal conservatives" within their own party.

To stake a horizontal position, as George W. Bush tried to do with this "compassionate conservatism," Republicans faced opposition from their colleagues who had grown understandably distrustful of the government's ability to enforce social justice. Given this mix of restraints and the left's near monopoly on the media, Republicans were thus routinely caricatured as heartless, racist, and xenophobic. The left publicly denounced the "religious right" as repressive zealots, and old line Republicans privately denounced them as political liabilities. Republicans seemed nearly as uncomfortable embracing the Agenda of the Lamb as the Democrats did.

Appearances, however, can be deceiving. In 2006, social scientist Arthur C. Brooks published a groundbreaking book on philanthropy titled *Who Really Cares*. What Brooks did was examine the real-life behavior of liberals and conservatives on the issue of compassion. Despite the stereotypes, the results were undeniable. Self-identified conservatives donate money to charity more often than self-identified liberals. They also donate a higher percentage of their incomes.[12]

Conservatives also donate more time to charity than do liberals. They even donate more blood. "If liberals and moderates gave blood at the same rate as conservatives," Brooks wrote, "the blood supply of the United States would jump about 45 percent."[13] So counter-instinctive were these findings that Brooks went back and recalculated his data to make sure he had not erred.

This much said, Republicans have a long way to go before they redeem the narrative of the cross. They must replace the image of an angry white evangelical bloc with a multiethnic, compassionate, truth-telling community. They must understand, no matter how patriotic they may be, that the cross trumps even the flag.

The Elephant must determine whether conservatism stands defined as the preservation and advancement of life, liberty, family, religious freedom, limited government, and free markets or the preservation of a monolithic voting constituency. In other words, the Elephant will make significant advances if it intentionally goes forward with the justice mission of Lincoln and the moral optimism of Ronald Reagan.

The difficulties are great. The media will ravage Republicans for publicly embracing the cross even if they do so with a strong social justice component. A second challenge is to build that component in such a way that it empowers the individual and does not further trap him or her in a lifetime of government dependence. It is possible to create a movement that integrates the vertical and horizontal planes of the cross, but it cannot be done without a little courage, a lot of character, and a major gift of divine guidance.

4.

RIGHTEOUSNESS
AND JUSTICE

HE WROTE THE LAW WITH ONE FINGER AND grace with both hands. The same God who pointed to righteousness via tablets of stone likewise imparted redemptive justice through the sacrifice on the cross. He is, after all, the God of righteousness and justice.

While there seems to be little debate on the definition of *righteousness* as an act of moral law, integrity, and rectitude, the word *justice* stands as one of the most exploited and perverted terms in our lifetime.

Before going further in this discussion, we must first ask ourselves, what exactly is justice? Although many operatives in the political sphere have tried to put their stamp on the word— social justice, economic justice, environmental justice—no one has copyrighted the term just yet. Nor will they ever. Justice does not belong to the left or to the right. Justice flows from on high for the purpose of lifting up the low.

What is justice? Justice is not the purpose of big government.

Justice is the passion of a big God. Justice is not a political term to be exploited but a prophetic term to be lived out. Justice does not result in pathetic attempts of expediency but in prophetic postures of activism.

What is justice? Justice will on occasion march, on other occasions protest, and yet on other occasions sing, but justice will always speak for those who cannot speak for themselves. Justice is spokesperson for the suffering, advocate for the poor, and father of the orphan.

What is justice? Justice flows not from the Donkey or the Elephant. Justice is given birth by the Lamb. For if the heart of God is called "righteousness," then his hand is called "justice." Justice is horizontal righteousness. Justice is righteousness applied.

For without righteousness, it is impossible even to imagine justice. Here lies the problem of our times. Many attempt to do justice without embracing righteousness. They fail to understand that the horizontal plane of the cross without the vertical looks like any other piece of wood on the floor.

If the Agenda of the Lamb is to be fulfilled, the cross movement demands both righteousness *and* justice, not *either/or*. Fortunately, there exists a generation within the church with the heart's desire to reconcile the two planes. This generation seeks a holistic gospel that looks up and looks around, with holy hands lifted high and helping hands stretched out.

For too long we have thought it possible, even useful, to separate these planes. Yet the very practice of separating righteousness from justice has the real-world effect of separating denominations, communities, and ethnicities from one another. In reality, there exists no such entity as a righteousness-only church or a justice-only church. There is only one true church, the church of Jesus Christ, and I assure the reader, the church does not suffer from bipolar disorder. It stands committed, as it always has, to righteousness and justice.

The words in Psalm 89:14 could not be clearer: "Righteousness and justice are the foundation of your throne. Unfailing love and truth walk before you as attendants" (NLT).

As stated previously, white Evangelicals in the twentieth century tended to focus on righteousness issues while black Evangelicals tended to focus on justice. If we are to engage this generation of North Americans with the message of salvation and transformation, we must engage both the vertical and horizontal planes within the spheres of life, church, community, and culture. We must present the Bible in the context of both eternal spiritual salvation through Christ and socially transformative outreach to Christ's people. And Christ's people, be reminded, include all of humanity.

If we are to engage this generation with the good news, we must reconcile the optics of redemption with the metrics of reconciliation. This generation seeks a cause. In its DNA one can find a passion for prophetic stewardship, but right now that passion is largely being squandered. Those who occupied Wall Street did so only until the first snows fell. Those who rallied at Tea Parties did so only until the results of the 2010 election came in. These were not—could not be—ends in themselves. Nor can environmentalism be an end in itself or feminism or radicalism or socialism or libertarianism or any other kind of "ism" for that matter.

The youth of this generation can satisfy that passion for justice through the Word. The inspired Word of God uniquely offers this generation a cause greater than itself. For that matter, the gospel of Jesus Christ stands as the manifesto for such a cause, the contextualized moral imperative for righteousness and justice.

With the Lamb's Agenda, this generation will reestablish righteousness and reclaim justice. It will rescue the justice narrative from the social engineers, the political manipulators, and the utopian materialists. It will free people from a dependency on government and inspire them toward a dependency on God.

With the Lamb's Agenda, the Christ-centered, Bible-believing church will once again emerge as the most transformative institution in every community. The church will be the catalyst for the change, the reconciler of communities, the one true unifying cause.

Parenthetically, one of the distinguishing features in Latin American culture was born in the initial commitment of the Spanish Crown in the early days of exploration. As the Spaniards built cities throughout Latin America, they committed to building a church in the center of each city. As a matter of fact, until this day, the very heart of Latin American cities from Argentina to Mexico and all points in-between can be reached by following the signage to the church.

The recent film, *For Greater Glory*—starring Andy Garcia, directed by Dean Wright, and produced by Pablo José Barroso—captures the centrality of Christianity to Latin American life. The movie tells the true story of the Cristero War, which unfolded in Mexico in the late 1920s.

At the time, Mexico's atheist president, Plutarco Elías Calles, began to implement strict anti-clerical laws. The clerics who resisted were, in many cases, imprisoned or killed. Calles, however, underestimated the depth of the people's commitment to Christianity and to religious freedom. The rebellion of the "Cristeros" attracted the world's attention.

On June 27, 1929, nearly three years after the rebellion began, the Mexican government relented, and church bells rang in

Mexico for the first time in almost three years. More than thirty thousand Cristeros died to make this happen. Kudos to the film-makers for bringing this inspirational story to life. Its arrival in America's movie theaters during the height of the debate over religious freedom seems more than a little providential.

Ironically, as California continues its mindless effort to drive all vestiges of Christ's legacy from the public square, it cannot divest itself of the names of its major cities, all of which were started as Spanish missions: Los Angeles, San Francisco, San Diego, Santa Barbara, and many more.

As we reconstruct the cross and restore the justice plane to its proper place, the church will once again emerge as the center of our communities. For there was a time when the homeless, the widow, the orphan, the addicted, and the unemployed depended more on the compassionate outreach of the church than on the condescension of Uncle Sam.

While our good uncle may assist in the outreach of justice, he cannot take the lead. Why? Uncle Sam is not anointed in the way of righteousness and justice. His workers do what they do for a paycheck, some with compassion in their hearts to be sure, but some without. Then, too, the people paying for those checks may not even believe in what the workers are doing. These tax-payers have little to no choice but to pay; the alternative to not paying is prison.

This system has its virtues, but they are not Christian vir-tues. "But love ye your enemies," Jesus said in Luke 6:35, "and do good, and lend, hoping for nothing again; and your reward shall be great, and ye shall be the children of the Highest: for he is kind unto the unthankful and to the evil" (KJV).

Christian socialists, occasionally even non-Christian social-ists, strive to make Jesus one of their own. They like to cite the many pleas of Jesus for charity and compassion and, if pushed to nationalize these gestures, cite one particular passage from Matthew 25:32. "All the nations will be gathered before him, and he will separate the people one from another as a shepherd separates the sheep from the goats."

The critical word above is *nations*. The argument is offered that Jesus smiles on those nation-states that direct their redistributive policies toward the "least of these my brethren." Although creative, this reading flies in the face of everything else voiced on this issue in both the Old and New Testaments. Nowhere in the Bible does Jesus, God the Father, Moses, the apostles, the prophets, or anyone of consequence argue that the faithful should cede the justice mission to a secular state. In every instance in the Bible, it is the individual, the community, the family, or the church that assumes the responsibility for taking care of the least of our brethren.

When governments assume control of the justice agenda, they can almost never restrain themselves from wanting more and more power. "Of all tyrannies," said C. S. Lewis sagely, "a tyranny sincerely exercised for the good of its victims may be the most oppressive."[1]

Josef Stalin proved Lewis's point. In 1928, Stalin launched a five-year plan to assure a more equal distribution of wealth among citizens of the Soviet Union. As a starter, he hoped to eradicate "all kulak tendencies." A "kulak" was originally defined as the equivalent of a "one percenter" in the jargon of Occupy Wall Street. These were the wealthy landowners who produced more than they were said to need.

By 1930, ever-increasing taxes had impoverished even the wealthy kulaks. Not satisfied, Stalin appropriated their property. He then started defining "kulak" to mean all property owners, including peasants, and forced them all into collectives. When the kulaks and peasants resisted, Stalin began an escalating series of arrests, deportations, and executions, and finally a ruthless plan of forced starvation.

When landowners continued to resist, Stalin sent in his troops to enforce the "ear law" (so called because a peasant could be arrested and executed for withholding any "socialist property" right down to an ear of corn). By the end of the five-year plan, there were at least five million dead, all of them killed in the name of social justice.[2]

The Soviet Union is an extreme case, but not that extreme. The experience of those living under Communism in China, Cuba, Cambodia, and other countries has been as bad or worse. Even in relatively enlightened socialist countries, religious faith is inevitably sacrificed to the growing power of the state. People lose confidence in their ability to make a difference. They stop having children. They live for themselves on a day-to-day basis. If a nation is to achieve real justice, compassionate and noncoercive justice, Christ's anointed followers must take the lead. We have seen many brilliant examples of this in the past.

WILLIAM WILBERFORCE

One man who demands special attention is the British abolitionist William Wilberforce. Wilberforce entered the British Parliament in 1784 as a slacker and a dandy. Through a series of providential encounters, however, he embarked upon what he called his "Great Change." A religious skeptic, Wilberforce began opening his mind after a lengthy conversation with a trusted friend. Bible study followed. Although polite society had little use for sincere believers, Wilberforce emerged from this period of reflection and study as a devout evangelical Christian.

Along the way, he met up with John Newton, a former slave trader turned pastor, who was also the writer of the classic hymn "Amazing Grace." After their meeting, Wilberforce wrote, "my mind was in a calm, tranquil state, more humbled, looking more devoutly up to God."[3] If this upward gaze represented the vertical plane of the cross, Newton encouraged Wilberforce to shoulder a horizontal one as well, namely the abolition of the slave trade. He believed that God had raised Wilberforce up "for the good of the nation."[4]

Unlike politicians whose passions come and go, Wilberforce championed this cause until his death nearly fifty years later. He was not in it to win votes but to serve the Lord. Indeed, only a deep devotion could have enabled him to fight as long as he did and to ignore the slights that came his way.

At the time, Britain was the world leader in that unholy trade. There were many vested interests to overcome and not only the economic ones. The British Royal Family had little use for abolition. Even Admiral Lord Nelson, Britain's greatest naval hero, violently rejected "the damnable doctrine of Wilberforce and his hypocritical allies."[5]

Success did not come easily. It would take Wilberforce and his colleagues twenty years to ban the slave trade in Britain and another twenty-five years after that to abolish slavery throughout the British Empire. "If to be feelingly alive to the sufferings of my fellow-creatures is to be a fanatic," said Wilberforce at the time, "I am one of the most incurable fanatics ever permitted to be at large."[6]

BILL WILSON

Bill Wilson was a drunk. He had his first taste of alcohol as a soldier during World War I and had a hard time staying sober during the following fifteen years. Ebby Thacher, a boyhood pal of Wilson's, was also a drunk. But through his involvement with the Oxford Group, a nondenominational movement based on first-century Christianity, he found the strength to stay sober.

In 1934, Thacher visited Wilson and convinced his friend that, based on his own experience, God could help him overcome his addiction. Although not a religious person, Wilson opened himself up to Thacher's message. Wilson wrote the following about his conversion experience:

> There (in the hospital) I humbly offered myself to God, as I then understood Him, to do with me as He would. I placed myself unreservedly under His care and direction. I admitted for the first time that of myself I was nothing; that without Him I was lost. I ruthlessly faced my sins and became willing to have my new-found Friend take them away, root and branch. I have not had a drink since.[7]

From the very beginning, Wilson understood the two-plane message of the cross. It was not enough to save himself through his personal experience with God. He had to reach out and help others. "Faith without works was dead," he would write. "And how appallingly true for the alcoholic! For if an alcoholic failed to perfect and enlarge his spiritual life through work and self-sacrifice for others, he could not survive the certain trials and low spots ahead."[8]

Wilson and Bob Smith, another recovering alcoholic, left the Oxford Group largely because the group failed to understand Wilson's horizontal outreach. The alcoholic benefited, Wilson thought, from a reliance on God and a communal relation with his fellow believers. In 1937, Wilson and a few colleagues wrote the book, *Alcoholics Anonymous: The Story of How More Than One Hundred Men Have Recovered from Alcoholism*. It would be from this book, "The Big Book," that the organization Wilson cofounded (Alcoholics Anonymous) drew its name.

Although Wilson did not make AA a Christ-centered organization, one senses Christ's hand behind it. Today there are more than one hundred thousand AA groups worldwide, and nearly two million members. It functions exactly as a godly philanthropy should. It has no leadership hierarchy, no political agenda, no lobbyists, no reliance on government funding. Wilson called AA a "benign anarchy."[9] Although AA is criticized both by those who think it too religious and those who think it not religious enough, it serves as a valuable model for how a believer can help solve a major societal problem as an outreach of Christian ministry without government intervention.

Martin Luther King Jr.

Martin Luther King has, of course, become a national icon, but it is useful to recall the profound Christian roots of his mission. Although an imperfect human being like the rest of us, King is among the greatest American models of the prophetic tradition. He moved on both the vertical and horizontal planes of the cross, emulating Christ both in life and in death.

Something of a skeptic as a child, King deepened his faith

through prayer and study, first at Crozer Theological Seminary in Pennsylvania and later at Boston University where he received his doctor of philosophy degree. As a pastor, he relied heavily on the Bible both for inspiration and for direction.

King came of age at a critical juncture in American history. At the time, there were any number of people and groups that aspired to lead the ascendant civil rights movement. But in his wisdom, God chose Martin Luther King Jr.

King drew much of his own wisdom from Jesus' famed Sermon on the Mount, which helped structure King's response to the violence that he knew his movement would inevitably face. He expressed his thoughts thusly:

> Returning hate for hate multiplies hate, adding deeper darkness to a night already devoid of stars. Darkness cannot drive out darkness: only light can do that. Hate cannot drive out hate: only love can do that. Hate multiplies hate, violence multiplies violence, and toughness multiplies toughness in a descending spiral of destruction. So when Jesus said, "Love your enemies," he is setting forth a profound and ultimately inescapable admonition. . . . The chain reaction of evil—hate begetting hate, wars producing more wars—must be broken, or we shall be plunged into the dark abyss of annihilation.[10]

One reason that King and the Southern Christian Leadership Conference could accomplish things that his secular peers in the Urban League or the NAACP could not was that he appealed to the same larger tradition that white American Christians also honored. "If we are wrong," King once said of his mission, "Jesus of Nazareth was merely a utopian dreamer that never came down to Earth."[11]

There is obviously a lot of unfinished business in regard to King's dream. There has been many a candidate, but no Christian of his stature to come along in the forty-five years since his death to carry his cross forward. That may change. We pray it does.

CHARLES COLSON

When Charles Colson entered Maxwell Correctional Facility for Watergate related crimes in Alabama in July 1974, no one, including perhaps Colson himself, could have anticipated the plan that God had in store for him. At the time, Colson was known as one of the most ruthless of Richard Nixon's lieutenants—a hatchet man. A quote by a Washington official that "Colson would walk over his own grandmother if he had to" would mutate into a quote by Colson saying that very thing himself. He never did, of course, but he gave every impression that he could have.

Indeed, when word of Colson's conversion to Christianity reached the press in 1973, the *Boston Globe* reported, "If Mr. Colson can repent of his sins, there just has to be hope for everybody."[12] There is, of course, hope for everybody, and Colson's post-Watergate life is a testament to the same.

In fact, Colson found his faith before prison. That faith inspired him to plead guilty and accept his fate. That fate became his calling. He could never forget the hopelessness and despair he saw in his fellow convicts. A year after his release, Colson began offering seminars for furloughed prisoners in Washington DC. When challenged by a warden to bring the programs inside the walls, Colson did just that.

This move opened the doors for hundreds of thousands of

prisoners around the world to receive biblically based teaching through seminars and Bible studies. It also impressed on Colson the need to train local volunteers to go inside prisons and work directly with inmates. In the years since, Colson's Prison Fellowship has grown to become the most extensive prison outreach service in the world, with a volunteer network of more than twenty thousand.

Colson was a modern-day Good Samaritan, one who stood committed to bringing good news to the poor and freedom to the captive. His concern for the incarcerated extended well beyond ministering to the spiritual needs of those in prison. Colson cared about their families outside the prison gates. His desire was to see the church not only engage the culture, but also reform it. An iconic figure, he enriched the Christian community by personifying the power of a redeemed narrative.

Not surprisingly, the prison ministry has faced opposition from the ideologues on the left. The same people who have succeeded in taking God out of schools now want to take God out of prisons. They are working through the courts to do just that despite the tangible benefits to society of transforming unrepentant criminals into practicing Christians.

"Christians should never have a political party," said Colson. "It is a huge mistake to become married to an ideology, because the greatest enemy of the gospel is ideology. Ideology is a man-made format of how the world ought to work, and Christians instead believed in the revealing truth of Scripture."[13]

Much to my great sorrow, Chuck Colson died shortly before *The Lamb's Agenda* was published. I had the privilege of serving with him on the Gordon Conwell Theological Seminary Board and serving as his Hispanic partner for the Manhattan Declaration—more on this later. He served as one of my greatest inspirations. His personal experience speaks of a man who fell into grace rather than falling from grace. From the birth of Prison Fellowship to the Manhattan Declaration, Dr. Colson's optics of reconciling truth with love permeated all aspects of his life. Although his physical voice may be silenced, his ideas and convictions will carry on by way of a generation committed to reconciling righteousness with justice.

As a result of his experiences, Colson became militantly pro-life. "The pro-life agenda has no meaning apart from its being rooted in absolute truth, in self-evident truths—truths that are true because they're true, not because somebody says they are true," said Colson.[14] As Colson implicitly understood, the Agenda of the Lamb requires reconciling a pro-life and pro-family platform with the quest for social justice—whether that quest leads the individual to prisoner outreach, civil rights work, care for the addicted, the fight against the slave trade (which continues to this day) or a score of other causes that flow naturally from the horizontal plane of the cross. It is impossible to adequately address these issues without a pro-life foundation.

Well-meaning people who collaborate on social issues with enemies of life usually find themselves betrayed. In 2006, Los Angeles Cardinal Roger Mahony learned this the hard way when he risked his reputation to cooperate with Dolores Huerta, cofounder of the United Farm Workers, and the leadership of the SEIU on the issue of illegal immigration. When the Catholic Church in Los Angeles was challenged on its collaboration with leftists hostile to the life issue, its leaders insisted, "This isn't about left or right. This is about justice."[15]

A few months later, the unions and Huerta repaid the Catholic Church for its support by disregarding organized labor's long-standing neutrality on the abortion issue and asking their members to reject Proposition 85. This proposition would merely have required underage girls to get parental permission before an abortion. As the *Los Angeles Times* noted, Huerta, "a Roman Catholic," had been instrumental in spreading the word to union members whose support would prove crucial in defeating Proposition 85 by a narrow 53 to 47 margin.[16] Unlike Huerta, late UFW founder César Chávez was a devout Catholic who based his social justice mission on the Christian tradition. He would have been appalled.

As Chávez understood, the nexus of righteousness and justice is life and family. Let me give a shout-out here to Steve Macías, west coast regional coordinator for Students of America for Life, who understands Chávez's heritage. Sierra College of California attempted recently to co-opt its César Chávez Speaker Series by promoting a radical, pro-abortion forum featuring abortion clinic managers and abortion advocates. Macías spoke out. A Mexican American from a Christian migrant-farm-working family, Macías protested the series because it promised to not only abuse taxpayer money but also to "dishonor the legacy of César Chávez."[17] Macías and his allies succeeded in this protest, and the university withdrew its support.

Let us be clear. Social justice begins with life. For without life one cannot embrace liberty, and without liberty it is impossible to pursue happiness. The quintessential civil rights issue of the twenty-first century is the protection of the unborn. Our justice platform must always begin with life.

Essentially, justice is nothing other than righteousness in action. Justice provides the answer to the query submitted by Christ in the now famous Good Samaritan parable, "Who is your neighbor?" The Agenda of the Lamb prompts us to respond with the following: My neighbor is the most vulnerable among us, and no one is more vulnerable than the child in the womb. Wilberforce found his neighbors in the stinking holds of slave ships. Bill Wilson found his in the skid rows and the drunk tanks. Martin Luther King found his in the cotton fields of the South and the ghettos of the North. Charles Colson found his neighbors in jail cells and prison yards. César Chávez found his amid the dust and insecticides of California's Imperial Valley.

As Christian leaders our response to this query speaks more about who we are rather than those to whom we will reach out. The question "Who is my neighbor?" tells me less about those around me than about who I am in the midst of a lost and dying world.

5.

RECONCILING BILLY GRAHAM WITH MARTIN LUTHER KING JR.

GOOGLE THE WORD *PRIDE* AND YOU WILL FIND close to seven million entries. Extract company names, books, productions, and works of art from the list and the digital portal affirms the myriad applications that accompany and embrace the womb of sinfulness.

Pride is not just an emotion or, as Thomas Aquinas stated in *Summa Theologica*, the root of every sin. Pride is the great motivator for fame and fortune in the twenty-first century. While humility lies dormant, hidden away in the closet of archaic virtues, pride strides down the catwalk dressed to the nines, a model for all to ogle and admire.

Pride did not emerge from the idea we call "America"—it is as old as Lucifer—but, undoubtedly, this anti-virtue is as American as apple pie. Pride embraced slavery, while humility gave birth to abolition. Pride segregated, while humility fought for unity. Pride condemned the innocent, while humility defended the vulnerable.

Pride spends, while humility shares. Pride seeks recognition, while humility seeks righteousness. Pride looks inward and says, "Believe in yourself." Humility looks upward and says, "Believe in something greater than self."

Pride stands tall and does things "my way." Humility kneels down, head bowed, and does things "his way." However, pride never stands alone. Pride flirts with envy, gluttony, lust, anger, greed, stubbornness, and sloth. Yet stubbornness always seems to draw closest.

Why do great empires fall? Why do massive corporations fail? Why do relationships collapse? Pride. Pride stands center stage, taking its bows, unaware that the applause is false and the run finished. Humility, meanwhile, waits patiently in the wings, knowing that when pride implodes from that lethal cocktail of self-love and self-loathing, grace will render a silent introduction.

Although pride permeates America's cultural landscape, good people continue to walk humbly in the way of the Lord, none more so than the Reverend Billy Graham.

BILLY GRAHAM AND THE VERTICAL MOVEMENT

"We just received confirmation, Billy will be arriving shortly. You will have a chance to interact and we will take a group photo. We don't know how long he will stay, therefore let us be good stewards of this time together," said John Huffman, board chair of *Christianity Today*, as he informed the board members gathering at the Cove in North Carolina of Billy Graham's visit.[1]

Since I was fourteen years old, the two most influential figures in my personal journey have been Billy Graham and Dr. Martin Luther King Jr. I remember that Sunday evening in my early teen years like it was yesterday. After watching a Billy Graham crusade and a subsequent special on Dr. King, I felt like my life's mission statement could write itself: reconcile the salvation message preached by Billy Graham with the justice message of Dr. King.

As I approached to shake Billy Graham's hand on that memorable day in North Carolina in the fall of 2011, I knew more than ever that this mission had been worth pursuing. Before me sat a man who had made history. He led an evangelical movement that changed the face of Christianity—and the world for that matter—like few other preachers have since the early apostles. Billy Graham not only preached the gospel, but he also led a movement. To do both is not easy. It takes great talent and even greater humility.

Graham's Christian commitment to the gospel of Jesus Christ prompted him to create the infrastructure and the leadership apparatus necessary to sustain a movement. Those looking for a model of a twenty-first-century righteousness and justice movement committed to the Agenda of the Lamb would do well to study the foundational framework provided by Dr. Graham.

Graham understood that every movement required three components for viable and sustainable longevity: messaging platforms, mobilization mechanisms, and measurement instruments. He then went about creating and refining the necessary institutions to accomplish his goals.

For the purpose of messaging, Graham founded *Christianity Today* in 1956. He had become increasingly concerned that mainline Protestantism, in opening itself to the world, had forgotten its roots. This opening editorial laid out Graham's mission:

> *Christianity Today* has its origin in a deep-felt desire to express historical Christianity to the present generation. Neglected,

slighted, misrepresented—evangelical Christianity needs a clear voice, to speak with conviction and love, and to state its true position and its relevance to the world crisis. A generation has grown up unaware of the basic truths of the Christian faith taught in the Scriptures and expressed in the creeds of the historic evangelical churches.[2]

For the purpose of mobilization, Graham turned to Youth for Christ and became its first full-time evangelist while still in his twenties. For the purpose of research and education, he helped revive and reorganize Gordon Conwell Theological Seminary. Graham understood the importance of reconciling the deliverables with the delivery mechanisms, the outcome with the process, and substance with form.

Yet, the striking simplicity of his message—salvation through Christ and Christ alone—revolutionized the public sphere. Billy espoused a message that in essence conveyed a simple truth: Christ is the hope of the world. As stadiums filled and millions heard the gospel for the first time, Billy Graham taught us the lesson of deliberate prophetic articulation: preach the Word in and out of season.

Laura Hillenbrand's recent bestseller, *Unbroken: a World War II Story of Survival, Resilience, and Redemption*, has introduced millions of Americans, many of them unsuspecting, to the inspirational message of Billy Graham. The book tells the true story of Louie Zamperini, an Olympic long-distance runner who comes back to America after surviving the most frightful horrors Word War II could offer.

Unable to overcome the trauma on his own, Zamperini turned to alcohol and yielded to despair. While Zamperini was out burning up the bar scene in Los Angeles, Graham, then just thirty-one, came to town with his small team. They set up a circus tent on the corner of Washington Boulevard and Hill. "He had a direct gaze," wrote Hillenbrand, "a stern jawline, and a southern sway in his voice, the product of a childhood spent on a North Carolina dairy farm." At first, the crowds were slim. But then, wrote Hillenbrand, "his blunt, emphatic sermons got people talking."[3]

Finally, at the repeated urging of a loving wife, Zamperini attended one of Graham's tent meetings. When Graham began to speak of how "darkness doesn't hide the eyes of God," Zamperini grew uneasy. Graham went on to say that on judgment day, the sinner would stand before God and watch his life play out on a screen before him, "And your own words, and your own thoughts, and your own deeds, are going to condemn you as you stand before God on that day."

Zamperini's pride rebelled, and he bolted from the tent. He was an Olympian, a war hero, a *bon vivant* who did things his way. " 'I am a good man,' he thought, 'I am a good man.' " His wife begged him to return another night. He relented, bolted again, only then to find his rage and humiliation melt away. Hillenbrand wrote, "That morning, he believed, he was a new creation. Softly, he wept."[4] Zamperini was one of more than three million people who found their way to Jesus through Billy Graham.

As a cultural postscript, although most reviewers were respectful given Hillenbrand's early success with her bestseller *Seabiscuit,* many of them refused to mention Graham, which is odd given that this was a tale, the subtitle tells us, "of redemption." Gary Krist was one such critic. "So what is it that enables a man to endure such trials and emerge unbroken?" wrote Krist in the *Washington Post.*[5] He seems not to have a clue as he makes no mention of Graham, God, or Jesus Christ.

In essence, Billy's success can be measured not only by what he preached and organized, but also by the actions he never took. He never changed his message to accommodate the changing times. He never sacrificed truth on the altar of political expediency and he never compromised personal integrity. Thus, the iconic leader of a movement demonstrated that the message and the messenger must be the same both on and off the pulpit. In this regard, Dr. Graham succeeded in modeling authentic movement leadership, where success is not measured by exuberance but rather by the metrics of integrity and humility.

Dr. King and the Horizontal Movement

The same year I met Billy Graham, I had the privilege of speaking at Ebenezer Baptist Church in Atlanta. I did not find it to be a coincidence that in the same year I shook the hand of my evangelistic / vertical hero, I also held the hand of Bernice King, the daughter of Dr. Martin Luther King Jr., my evangelistic / horizontal hero, as she escorted me through her father's childhood home.

We spoke about her father, his dream, and his faith. I learned that successful movements require leaders who rise up with the gift of speaking the dream. King had that gift. He mastered the art of prophetic and persuasive articulation that engages the heart, head, and hand. When King spoke, you heard both the doctoral degree from Boston University and the polished preacher from Atlanta.

Dr. King often made reference to a "journey." Using the metaphorical and prophetic application of biblical narratives, he spoke of a people that would make it to the promised land. King knew that to overcome segregation he had to use language that spoke not just to the intellect but to the *nephesh*—the living, breathing soul of man.

King spoke the language of deliverance and freedom. In essence, he saw in America the day when the marginalized would leave the desert of despair and hopelessness and step into the land of hope and opportunity. As we seek to reconcile Billy Graham's vertical message with Dr. King's prophetic activism, we must ask, did Dr. King's dream become a reality?

I have no doubt that we've come a long way in our nation. We've come a long way from Egypt; we're no longer making bricks without straw. We've come a long way from the days of captivity, government endorsed racism, and the abomination of slavery. Thank God that Egypt is in our past.

We've come a long way, America. We've come a long way from the desert of Jim Crow and segregation. We've come a long way from the bombing of 16th Street Baptist and the dogs unleashed against innocent protesters. We've come a long way from the desert. Yes, we've come a long way. While we're not where we used to be, let us acknowledge the fact that there is still a long way to go. We're not done yet. We're just getting started.

I believe as Dr. King prophesied that we have entered the promised land. We have crossed the River Jordan. We have carried the ark and we have carried the glory. We have set that first foot on the land of milk and honey, scouted about, and savored the potential. How did we do it? How did we cross? How did we overcome? We overcame not by fear, discord, or discontent. We overcame by the blood of the Lamb.

Yet, while the days of slavery and Jim Crow are behind us, there remains a legacy of distrust, disharmony, despair, and brokenness. We may have entered the promised land, but as the ancient Israelites discovered, that land was not free from strife.

There were giants about in the land, and there are giants in ours. There's work to be done when today in America millions of children do *not* embrace life, understand liberty, or pursue the joys that lead to lasting happiness.

There's work to be done when thirty million people live in poverty. There's work to be done when unmarried teens get pregnant, men abandon their roles as fathers, pornography seduces technology, God is mocked, sin is embraced, relativism abounds, and Sunday remains the most segregated day of the week. There is work to be done. There's work to be done when pushers are more admired than preachers, school grounds look like battlegrounds, and our neighbors sit paralyzed by the gate called Beautiful, begging for change. There's work to be done.

For that matter, a righteousness and justice movement committed to the Agenda of the Lamb can serve as the facilitative platform for a Christ-centered, Bible-based, vertical and horizontal movement that will address the work before us. Billy Graham and Martin Luther King had many things in common, but one shared belief stands out: they both had confidence that the same God who started the good work would finish that work.

Anointed Oracles of Righteousness and Justice

Dr. King engaged in what can best be described as prophetic activism. He understood that biblical narratives ignite a spiritual flame that informs, inspires, and imparts a sense of urgency. Dr. King was a Christian, a preacher, a civil rights leader, an organizational executive, a Nobel Peace Prize recipient, but he was more than that; he was anointed.

This divine empowerment, shared by Billy Graham and Dr. King alike, serves as the distinguishing resource enabling both Graham and King to speak with such eloquence, grace, and authority. Correspondingly, a Lamb's Agenda movement can only succeed if the oracles of righteousness and justice speak truth with love, conviction with compassion, and a catalytic message with an undeniable anointing.

We need anointed voices to arise in our nation, from Main Street to Wall Street, from the barrio to Beverly Hills, from Washington DC to Washington State. Everywhere and anywhere, we need the oracles of righteousness and justice to arise. A Lamb's Agenda righteousness and justice movement requires anointed spokesmen and spokeswomen to stand up in each village, each town, and each city in our nation and be heard.

For God anoints whom he appoints. God anointed Moses to deliver the Hebrew children out of Egypt. He anointed Joshua to knock down the walls of Jericho. He anointed David to defeat the giant called Goliath. He anointed Elijah to silence the false prophets. He anointed Jesus to break the bondage of sin and give us life everlasting.

Once again the Spirit of God is in the anointing. As I travel around our nation and speak before students in colleges and universities, I am convinced that God is pouring out a fresh anointing upon a generation.

God is anointing a generation that will deliver our brothers and sisters from malnourishment and hunger, as well as from physical and spiritual poverty. He is anointing a generation to knock down the walls of racial and economic injustice. He is anointing a generation to defeat the unholy giants of abortion, human trafficking, and violence. He is anointing a generation that will silence the false prophets of discord, fear, terror, and hopelessness. As we learn in Isaiah 61:1, God is anointing a generation to declare:

> *The Spirit of the Sovereign LORD is on me,*
> *because the LORD has anointed me*
> *to proclaim good news to the poor.*
> *He has sent me to bind up the brokenhearted,*
> *to proclaim freedom for the captives*
> *and release from darkness for the prisoners.*

MARRYING THE MESSAGE WITH THE MARCH

Reconciling Graham with King will enable the followers of Christ to lead the proverbial march for righteousness and justice. While the majority of Christ-centered, Bible-based communities did not participate in the civil rights movement of the twentieth century, the Lamb's Agenda will catapult this same community to the forefront of a twenty-first-century Christian civil rights movement, one that will protect life, preserve family, and defend religious liberty. Silence, apathy, and complacency will not prevail—not this time around.

We followers of the Lamb's Agenda must never again stand on the sidelines as injustice subverts our nation and our church. Never again can we hide under the cloak of political correctness. Never again can we ignore the plight of the suffering, the persecuted, and the marginalized. Never again can we suffer from vertical or horizontal myopia. Never again can we separate the message from the march.

A few months ago I received a call alerting me that Planned Parenthood was building the largest abortion complex in the

Western Hemisphere in a Houston neighborhood primarily inhabited by Hispanics and African Americans. In a matter of fourteen days, we assisted in gathering close to twenty thousand marchers—black, white, Asian, and Latino—to demonstrate opposition to an industry deliberately targeting communities of color. Indeed, a black unborn baby is three times more likely to die in the womb than a white. It is no accident that so many abortion mills dot the inner city. They prey on the most vulnerable.

As we began to march toward the abortion complex, we drew inspiration from Dr. King and we began our march for life and justice singing an old African American spiritual:

> *We shall overcome*
> *We shall overcome*
> *We shall overcome one day*
> *Deep in my heart I do believe*
> *We shall overcome one day*

What America needs is a generation committed to marrying the evangelistic message of Billy Graham with the prophetic activism of Dr. King. One woman who has done just that is Dr. King's niece Alveda King. "Abortion and racism are both symptoms of a fundamental human error," said Alveda. "The error is thinking that when someone stands in the way of our wants, we can justify getting that person out of our lives. Abortion and racism stem from the same poisonous root, selfishness."[6]

A pastor and an activist, Alveda has fearlessly taken her uncle's mission to the nation's abortion industry. I say "fearlessly" not just because this industry is willing and able to lash back. I say "fearlessly" because in taking up this crusade Alveda has alienated many in the black community more attached to the Donkey than to the cross. Even the most loving follower of the Lamb's Agenda will make enemies.

The challenge is to make converts out of enemies. To do this, we need a generation that will reconcile the message with the march, the Way with the Dream, the call for salvation with a call for justice, and the song of redemption with the song of deliverance. Reconciling King with Graham will bring together urban and suburban, the white and the black, covenant and community, righteousness and justice. When this happens, this new generation of Christ followers will proudly sing both "We Shall Overcome" and "Room at the Cross for You."[7]

This renewed fervor will demonstrate to the world that, in America, hope and faith still thrive in the lives of the young who call themselves "Followers of Christ." These are the ones willing to accompany Billy Graham to the cross and to sit with Dr. King at the Master's table. For we indeed shall overcome one day.

6.

RECONCILING JOHN 3:16 WITH MATTHEW 25

WE SHOULD NOT BE TALKING RIGHT NOW. According to the naysayers who predicted Christianity's demise by the year 2000, we should not even be here.

In 1917 Communist officials declared in St. Petersburg, Russia, that by the twenty-first century the entire world would embrace Communism, and the Christian faith would cease to exist. In the 1930s the Nazi regime declared that they would outlast the followers of Jesus. In the 1960s, rock musicians—"We're more popular than Jesus now"—boasted that by the turn of the century they would receive more praise and adulation than the Father, Son, and Holy Ghost combined.

We are well into the twenty-first century. Lenin is entombed; the Third Reich is dead; The Beatles are gone, but the church of Jesus Christ is still alive and well! Why do we continue to grow, even in the midst of adversity and persecution? Simply stated, we thrive because we are centered. We are centered in a way no other movement can be. We have Christ as the center of our church.

77

For the Agenda of the Lamb to go forward, we must secure the centrality of Christ. This we must do deliberately and consistently. On that first Good Friday the cross of Christ stood high on Calvary, visible to all coming and going—inescapable, central. Jesus was not then and cannot now be on the periphery. Jesus is always central.

Any movement without Christ at the center stands doomed to slow, sputter, and eventually fail. Christ provides the way, the truth, and the life of every transformative exercise imaginable. Incorporating Christ as part of a movement, a "component," does not suffice. The Lamb's Agenda requires all actions, all campaigns, all initiatives, and all efforts to spring from the message of Christ, crucified and resurrected.

A CHRIST-CENTERED MOVEMENT

Who do they say I am? Who do you think I am? (Matthew 16:13–19)

> When Jesus came to the region of Caesarea Philippi, he asked his disciples, "Who do people say the Son of Man is?"
>
> They replied, "Some say John the Baptist; others say Elijah; and still others, Jeremiah or one of the prophets."
>
> "But what about you?" he asked. "Who do you say I am?"
>
> Simon Peter answered, "You are the Messiah, the Son of the living God."
>
> Jesus replied, "Blessed are you, Simon son of Jonah, for this was not revealed to you by flesh and blood, but by my Father in heaven. And I tell you that you are Peter, and on this rock I will build my church, and the gates of Hades will not overcome it. I will give you the keys of the kingdom of

heaven; whatever you bind on earth will be bound in heaven, and whatever you loose on earth will be loosed in heaven."

This biblical passage captures one of the most transformative moments in human history. Peter revealed Jesus. Jesus revealed the church, activated the purpose, and emancipated the kingdom. Revelation always leads to activation, and activation always leads to emancipation. We need a revelation of Jesus to activate our purpose as we lead a righteousness and justice movement. The Lamb's Agenda is nothing other than the agenda of Christ.

The Agenda of the Lamb demands a response to the query Christ laid before us two thousand years ago: "Who do they say I am?" Jesus was not seeking affirmation of his brand; he was not launching a multi-tier marketing arrangement; he was definitely not fretting about his reputation, or the management thereof. Rather, as often with Jesus' queries, this question would reveal more about the responder than the inquirer. *Who do they say I am?*

That first query is immediately followed by another: "Who do *you* say I am?" Those paying attention—then or now—cannot answer one question without answering the other. Of the two, the second question—"Who do *you* say I am?"—is much more important than the first. How we respond to the second question will determine how the world responds to the first. For if we do not know who Jesus Christ is, how will the rest of humanity ever know? The church must know who Christ is in order for the world to know who Christ is.

IDENTITY MORATORIUM

Today, Christ is still asking, "Who does the world say I am? Who do you—that is, the church—say I am?" By and large, the world seems to give Christ good reviews. Almost no one speaks ill of him. Many try to claim him, co-opt him, make him one of their own. Christ is seen as a revolutionary, a great philosopher, a liberator, a leader in the transformative tradition of Gandhi, Buddha, and Confucius. In Islam, Jesus Christ is considered to be a messenger of God. He is mentioned more in the Koran (twenty-five times) than Mohammad is. Muslims are required to believe in Jesus.

What the Muslims do not believe, what others who would use Jesus for their own purposes do not believe, is that Jesus is God, the savior who was sent to redeem the world. Yet on multiple occasions Jesus claimed, in fact, that he is God. "Very truly I tell you," he said in John 8:58, "before Abraham was born, I am!" Or, as Jesus said in Revelation 22:13, "I am the Alpha and the Omega, the First and the Last, the Beginning and the End." If Jesus is not God, then he is a fraud, not the noble wise man non-Christians, and even some lukewarm Christians, think him to be.

Why is the world not calling Christ "the Messiah"? For starters, the church conveys a mixed message regarding the identity of Christ. It suffers from what some would call an "identity moratorium." In other words, the church and its members refrain from choosing an identity and instead shop around among the apparent options.

Too many in our church pulpits have taken a moratorium on Christian identity. Simply put, the church is not responding as Peter did. He said, "You are Christ, the Messiah, the Son of the Living God." Unfortunately, this is not the message coming from the pulpits today. The popular, politically correct American church is saying to Christ, "You are the one who makes us feel good. You are the one who makes us rich. You are the one who understands my pain." The church presents Christ as the therapist, the bank, the philosopher, the friend, the hippie, the social activist, the look-the-other-way, zero-accountability, spiritual figure.

We see the results of identity crisis all around us. Our citizens, including many self-identified Christians, worry more about raising the debt ceiling than firming up our moral foundation. They concern themselves more with helping their kids find a good college than helping them find Christ. They fret more about their savings accounts than they do about their salvation.

Why is the American collective confused about Jesus? Simply stated, the church, our church, has not set them straight. Today's current moral and cultural malaise derives from a distorted message of who Christ is. It is, however, not too late to correct that message. It never is. We can live out the Agenda of the Lamb as well as we ever could, but to do so we must reintroduce Jesus. Not the Sunday morning TV feel-good Jesus, not the politically correct Jesus, not the loving hippie Jesus, not the wise philosopher Jesus.

When Jesus asks today, "Who am I?" it is time for a church of Peters to stand up and shout, "You are the Christ—the anointed one!" We need not only to tell the world Christ is the anointed one. We need to remind them of that again and again.

Anointed to do what? Christ is not only anointed. He is the *anointing.* He brings good news to the poor, freedom to the captive, sight to the blind, words to the mute, hearing to the deaf. Christ brings good news, and he is good news. The Agenda of the Lamb is his good news. We must remember that. We must find the positive, even in the negative, and preach that. For too long, the secular media have successfully painted Bible-believing followers of Christ as naysayers. According to them, all we do is oppose, oppress, and object.

We know this is not true, but we need to convince the world that it is not. Our narrative should be full of optimism, rich with compassion, brimming over with hope. Let us re-introduce Jesus as the way to glory. Let us distinguish him from the clutter.

Only Jesus is the Christ, only Jesus is the Messiah. As we learn in Acts 4:12, "Salvation is found in no one else, for there is no other name under heaven given to mankind by which we must be saved." Jesus is not just a counterculture revolutionary, and he is not a hippie on a cross. He is the Messiah. He is the Light of the world. He is the Word made flesh. He is the way, the truth, and the life. He is the Messiah, conqueror, Son of man and Son of God. He is the Alpha and Omega, King of kings, Lord of lords, and Host of hosts.

When asked, Peter did not identify Christ as the son of *a* god or a *dying* god. No, Peter declared Jesus "the Son of the Living God." Why did Peter not just say "the Son of God?" Why did he have to add an extra modifier? The Holy Spirit directed his answer. Peter said *living*. This is critical.

The Holy Spirit, acting through Peter, wanted the world to know that Christ is the Son of the *living* God. This was not some dead, buried, marble statue, museum-type God, but the living God.

If he is a living God, what kind of church should we be? What kind of Christians should we be? What kind of families should we grow? What kind of language should we speak? What kind of thoughts should we have? What kind of life should we live? Jesus tells us, "I have come that they may have life, and have it to the full" (John 10:10).

We stand surrounded by a culture of death and dying: dying communities, dying economies, dying families, dying faith, dying morals, dead dreams. Everything seems to be dying around us.

Yet the Lamb's Agenda sparks life. It is time to celebrate the living. America, we are here to reintroduce you not just to any god, but to the *living* God, a living gospel in a living church.

In the critical passage above, Jesus looked at Peter and said, "Blessed are you, Simon son of Jonah, for this was not revealed to you by flesh and blood, but by my Father in heaven. And I tell you that you are Peter, and on this rock I will build my church."

You see, when we reveal who God is in our life, God reveals to us our true identity. Typically, we get it all backward. We are inclined to pray, "If you fix my life, if you fill my life, then I will serve you." No, if we follow him, call upon him, grab hold of him, then he will reveal our true purpose. We must go first. If we reveal him, he will reveal us. If we praise him, he will pull us out. If we lift him up, he will lift us up. When we reveal the Christ, he reveals the Christ purpose in us.

Upon the revelation of Jesus as Christ and the Son of the Living God, Jesus said, "I will build my church, and the gates of Hell will not overcome it." The *gates of hell* will not, cannot, shall not, may not prevail, defeat, obstruct, overcome, or conquer the church of Jesus Christ! This cross-contextualized, church-led movement will only succeed if Christ is reintroduced in America as the Son of the Living God. It is time to stop praying for God to come down and to start telling the church to rise up.

We all need to be outspoken about Christ. For without Christ, it is impossible to reconcile the vertical with the horizontal. But with Christ, all things are possible. Working through the Lamb's Agenda we embrace the reality that we are baptized with Christ in Romans, crucified with Christ in Galatians, seated with Christ in Ephesians, strengthened by Christ in Philippians, hidden in Christ in Colossians, and ruling and reigning with Christ in Revelation.

For at the end of day, the Lamb's Agenda will propose to the nation one simple glorious prospect—hope. Not "hope" the campaign slogan, not "hope" a term of rhetorical expediency, but Christ the hope of glory, hope incarnated by the realization of an eternal truth.

A JOHN 3:16 MOVEMENT

New York Jets quarterback Tim Tebow often etches the citations of Bible verses into the eye black he wears during daytime football games. Among his favorites is John 3:16: "For God so loved the world that he gave his one and only Son, that whoever believes in him shall not perish but have eternal life." A generation ago, an athlete who proudly proclaimed his love for Christ would scarcely attract attention. That is not so true today.

As I mentioned earlier, if the percentage of Americans that attends church faithfully has remained stable, the percentage that rejects Christianity altogether has increased dramatically. Many of them are vocal and well placed in the media. Today, to proclaim your faith openly is to open yourself up to ridicule. After Buffalo beat Denver, with Tebow as quarterback, in December 2011, comedian Bill Maher tweeted the following to his hundreds of thousands of followers: "Wow, Jesus just . . . Tim #Tebow bad! And on Xmas Eve! Somewhere in hell Satan is Tebowing, saying to Hitler 'Hey, Buffalo's killing them.'"[1] By "tebowing," he meant kneeling down in prayer. Maher said this, of course, with no loss to reputation or income.

After Denver had won its sixth straight game with Tebow at the helm, Saturday Night Live chose to commemorate the win streak with a skit. After thanking his teammates, the skit's

Tebow character said, as Tebow himself might have, "I gotta thank the most important person in my life, my Lord and savior Jesus Christ because I could not do this without him. Thank you, Jesus!"

In the skit, however, a Jesus character showed up in the locker room. Misunderstanding why Tebow or anyone prays before a football game, the SNL writers presumed it must be for victory and so the Jesus character made slight of that. The real dagger, though, was reserved for Tebow's overt display of his love of Christ. Jesus finds that display off-putting. "Ok, all right, just take it down a notch, will you buddy?" the Jesus character scolded Tebow before departing. "Ok, not a command, just a request."[2]

The media are more tolerant of those Christians—certain politicians come to mind—who do not take their faith seriously. Those who do, whether they are athletes or politicians or movie stars, open themselves to ridicule or worse. Tebow, however, remains undaunted. As he told a Texas congregation on Easter 2012, "My biggest prayer is to kind of make that cool again, for a high school kid to get on a knee and pray, and it's not something that's unique or different and that it's O.K. to be outspoken about your faith."[3]

Those who follow the Tebow family know that Tim's faith is not just vertical and certainly not just for show. He was born in the Philippines, in Mindanao to be precise, where his father, Bob, did mission work. Tim's mother, Pam, contracted amoebic dysentery during the pregnancy, and the medicines she took threatened her unborn baby. Doctors advised her to abort the child, but the Tebows rejected his advice. Years later, Tim and Pam would go on to do a very subtle pro-life ad that aired during the 2010 Super Bowl.

Not surprisingly, the "controversial" ad provoked the frenzied wrath of the abortion rights crowd before they even saw it. "An ad that uses sports to divide rather than to unite has no place in the biggest national sports event of the year—an event designed to bring Americans together," said the president of the Women's Media Center, a theme that was echoed by many others.[4] This organization conspired with other powerful pressure groups to have CBS ban the ad.

CBS did not relent. Its executives had seen the script, and they knew how unobjectionable it was:

> **PAM TEBOW:** I call him my miracle baby. He almost didn't make it into this world. I remember so many times when I almost lost him. It was so hard. Well he's all grown up now, and I still worry about his health. Everybody treats him like he's different, but to me, he's just my baby. He's my Timmy, and I love him.
>
> **TIM TEBOW:** Thanks mom. Love you too.[5]

By protesting so vigorously, abortion rights advocates unwittingly made certain that millions more would see the ad and talk about it than if they had simply ignored it. God works in strange and mysterious ways.

At fifteen, Tebow was finally old enough to make his first mission trip to the Philippines, and he was thrilled at the opportunity. "That's how we were raised," he remembered, "with a joy in getting to tell people about Jesus." By this age, he also understood "how important it is to help those who are less fortunate."[6]

The particular project that attracted Tim and his family to the Philippines was an orphanage, started by Bob Tebow and named "Uncle Dick's Home," after family friend and benefactor, the late Dick Fowler. The plan laid out by the Bob Tebow

Evangelistic Association fits comfortably at the nexus of the cross. "The rapid growth of materialism threatens the future responsiveness to the Gospel," reads the Plan. "If we do not act now, while the Spirit is moving, this great harvest of souls could be lost forever."[7]

The Tebows meld the vertical and the horizontal, evangelism and compassion. One gets the sense that the real future of the church in America and around the world lies in just such an arrangement.

THE POWER OF COMPASSION

In August 1969, twelve-year-old Hal Donaldson learned how quickly one's security can vanish when the car his parents were driving smashed head-on into one driven by a drunk driver. Hal's father was killed, his mother rendered immobile, unable to work or even cook for her four children.

Hal and his three younger siblings got a quick life's lesson in both privation and compassion. People from local churches kicked in to help them with food and shelter until their mother could recover. They also befriended the kids and treated them like their own. This was a lesson that Hal would build his life around. "God was faithful," said Donaldson of the tragedy's aftermath. "He knit us together as a family."

Donaldson attributes the family's perseverance to his mom, "a praying mother." "She would not allow us to become bitter," Donaldson noted. She also insisted that, with God's help, they could determine their own future. Each of them did this successfully.

After studying journalism and then the Bible, Donaldson

was working in Northern California where he grew up helping small churches through an organization called "Church Care America." He recalled driving down a California highway when God told him, "Help those churches reach out to the poor and suffering."

Soon thereafter he made a trip to Calcutta on a writing project, and there he got to meet Mother Teresa. When she asked what he was doing to help the poor and suffering, he did not yet have a good answer. He decided it was time to find one. *I've got to do something,* he thought.

Donaldson started with a single pick-up truck and a load of food. He took it to a nearby migrant workers camp and shared with them a very simple message, "Jesus loves you. I love you. There is a church that loves you too."

"The Convoy of Hope started with a single pick-up truck," said Donaldson with a smile, "but God saw a fleet of semis." In the beginning, the Convoy was strictly local. Donaldson and his associates organized citywide outreach events that featured grocery giveaways, job fairs, and gospel presentations.[8]

Although the Convoy of Hope continues to do outreach programs in the United States, usually about fifty a year, Donaldson quickly realized the greatest need lies beyond our borders. Today, less than twenty years after Donaldson founded the organization, the Convoy of Hope feeds more than one hundred thousand children in seven nations. Its workers also provide clean and safe water in these communities, teach improved agricultural techniques, and help provide healthy living environments and education.

Donaldson sensed that organizations run by governments or the United Nations could not be as effective as one motivated by the love of God. The very mission of Convoy of Hope minimizes waste and all but eliminates corruption. Year after year, the organization gets high marks for its low overhead, high efficiency mobilization of tens of thousands of volunteers for community outreach, and disaster response work.

With God's help, the organization now has a US-based 300,000-square-foot distribution center, six international distribution centers, a fleet of trucks in multiple countries, more than 23,000 churches and organizations involved, more than 1,200 volunteer teams, nearly $300 million of gifts in kind to date, and more than 350,000 volunteers mobilized. In all, Convoy of Hope has helped more than 33 million people.

Through all this, Hal Donaldson has maintained the balance between the horizontal plane of community outreach and the vertical plane of staying grounded in Christ. "Our quest in life is to emulate Jesus," said Donaldson. He likes to cite the encounter between Jesus and the blind man in John, chapter 9, which holds some interesting lessons.

When the disciples asked Jesus who sinned that this man should have been born blind, the man himself or his parents, Jesus answered, "Neither this man nor his parents sinned, but this happened so that the works of God might be displayed in him." In other words, those who suffer may not have done anything to deserve their suffering. Nor is their suffering pointless. In this case, the man was born blind "so that the works of God might be displayed in him."

As the Pharisees learn of the cure, some among them grumbled about Jesus, "This man is not from God, for he does not keep the Sabbath." When the blind man insisted that Jesus was a godly man, the Pharisees erupted, "You were steeped in sin at birth; how dare you lecture us!" They then threw him out of the synagogue. Early on Donaldson rejected this kind of overly formal religiosity as it allowed tradition to trump compassion when the two seemed to be in conflict.

What Donaldson most appreciates about this story, however, is that Jesus was not content with curing the blind man's physical ills. He later sought him out. "Do you believe in the Son of Man?" Jesus asked him. "Lord, I believe," said the man, and he proceeded to worship Jesus. There is a necessary link, Donaldson argues, between compassion and evangelism. Each loses value without the other. Another verse that helps clarify his mission is Matthew 5:16, "In the same way, let your light shine before others, that they may see your good deeds and glorify your Father in heaven."

The Convoy of Hope addresses both the spiritual roots and social consequences of human suffering. It has succeeded because it follows Jesus' revolutionary model. Jesus embraced the banished, forgave those tormented by guilt, liberated those oppressed by evil spirits, and fed the hungry. His life was the cross in action, both planes of it, vertical and horizontal.

When we help the poor and oppressed, God blesses us and those we help. Speaking about King Josiah, God declares in Jeremiah 22:16, "He defended the cause of the poor and so all went well with him. Isn't that what it means to know me?"

Yes, Lord, it is.

A MATTHEW 25 MOVEMENT

There is much to learn from Matthew 25:

> Then the King will say to those on his right, "Come, you who
> are blessed by my Father; take your inheritance, the kingdom

prepared for you since the creation of the world. For I was hungry and you gave me something to eat, I was thirsty and you gave me something to drink, I was a stranger and you invited me in, I needed clothes and you clothed me, I was sick and you looked after me, I was in prison and you came to visit me."

Then the righteous will answer him, "Lord, when did we see you hungry and feed you, or thirsty and give you something to drink? When did we see you a stranger and invite you in, or needing clothes and clothe you? When did we see you sick or in prison and go to visit you?"

The King will reply, "Truly I tell you, whatever you did for one of the least of these brothers and sisters of mine, you did for me." (verses 34–40)

What are we anointed to do? Are we anointed to build great cathedrals? Are we anointed to build multimillion-dollar ministry platforms? Are we anointed to gather thousands around us to make them feel good about themselves and give them some place to go on Sunday mornings before brunch?

I don't think so. We are anointed to bring good news to the poor, freedom to the captive, and healing to the brokenhearted. In Matthew 25, Christ admonishes us to feed the hungry and clothe the needy.

Yet today, unfortunately, American Christendom too often measures success by the metrics of rows filled, books sold, and dollars collected rather than by the number of souls transformed. To recalculate our metrics, we need to ask ourselves, how does God measure success? The answer is simple and can be found in Matthew 25.

The Lamb's Agenda reconciles John 3:16 with Matthew 25.

Any church or Christian ignoring the plight of their neighbors lives an incomplete gospel. The Lamb's Agenda is both covenant and community, sanctification and service, orthodoxy and orthopraxy. Our vertical salvation must lead to horizontal transformation.

Accordingly, the good news must not only be preached, it must also be lived out. How do we live out the Lamb's Agenda? We read Matthew and we heed it. We read John 3:16 and acknowledge it. We recognize that the vision for any viable twenty-first century outreach melds covenant and community. Our vertical covenant propels us to stand as salt and light in our community.

We cannot easily justify a Christian ministry that convenes on Sunday morning and ignores its community from Monday through Saturday. Nor can we easily justify a ministry that treats Sunday like just another day to do good in the community. We derive our influence in that community not from our ability to plan events and schedule speakers, not from our eagerness to distribute food and fix houses. We derive our influence from our source of enlightenment and our willingness to share that light with those around us.

The good we do in the community must flow from a power beyond us. Governments can give out more food than we can, celebrities can draw more people, but only we can share the light of God in every good deed we do. We stand committed to a radical gospel message that marries sanctification with service, one that stands for biblical truth while putting the truth to work for the community.

7.

A KINGDOM CULTURE MOVEMENT

THIS NEXT GREAT VERTICAL AND HORIZONTAL righteousness and justice movement will not be a white, black, or brown movement, but rather a kingdom culture, multiethnic movement.

Notice how I did not say multicultural but multiethnic. The "culture" we all share—or can share—is God's kingdom culture. We can share in it whether we are black, white, or brown, or whether we are Americans, Egyptians, or Greeks.

I believe the greatest affirmation of our diversity derives from the sustainable enrichment of that kingdom culture. Without that greater sharing, diversity can easily lead to disintegration as we saw in the breakup of countries such as Yugoslavia and the Soviet Union, or even as we see in the gang wars and race riots of our own cities.

Looking at the world through a kingdom culture lens will enable us to see it much more richly than we do right now. When I wake up in the morning what I see first is not that I am Hispanic, black, white, or Asian; Republican or Democrat, conservative or liberal; charismatic or automatic; but rather that I am, first and foremost, a child of the living God. I don't see rivals. I don't see enemies. I see brothers and sisters. Ideally, they will see me as I see them.

VERTICAL IDENTITY EMPOWERING HORIZONTAL REALITY

In looking through the kingdom culture lens, I see the world around me as a stage of opportunity, a stage on which mercy, compassion, renewal, and hope hold forth; a stage on which truth becomes our moniker, charity our beacon, and justice our aspiration.

Pentecost stands as the quintessential marker of that cross-cultural, multilingual, spiritual movement. Until that moment, people of every culture saw those outside their culture as strangers. When the Jews looked beyond their borders, they saw the dread Samaritans, the accursed Canaanites, and the hated Philistines. When the Athenians looked beyond theirs, they saw barbarians, a word derived from the Greek word for foreign, *barbaros*. When the Romans looked beyond their borders, they saw fresh tribes to be conquered and exploited. After pentecost, when the followers of Christ looked beyond their borders, they saw new brothers and sisters in Christ. This was revolutionary.

To be sure, Christ's call to see strangers as friends wars with some of the darker instincts of human nature. Those calling themselves "Christians" have done some serious injustice to their fellow humans over time, but never have they done so at the urging of Christ. Nowhere in the Gospels is there a call to exclude, to ostracize, to hate, to fight. Indeed, just the opposite is true. As

Paul said to Timothy, "That is why we labor and strive, because we have put our hope in the living God, who is the Savior of all people, and especially of those who believe" (1 Timothy 4:10).

Just before ascending to heaven, as noted in Acts 1:8, Jesus said to his disciples, "But you will receive power when the Holy Spirit comes on you; and you will be my witnesses in Jerusalem, and in all Judea and Samaria, and to the ends of the earth." The Holy Spirit did indeed descend on Christ's disciples, and the nations, the tribes, the cultures of the world heard the good news of the gospel, "to the ends of the earth." No one was to be denied the good news. This included the Samaritans, the sinners, the shunned, the suffering.

Today, more than ever, we need a kingdom culture revolution in the church to revive the spirit of the pentecost and to remind us of its meaning. We need a heavenly outpouring, a *kairos* moment, which will enable us to speak the language of the communities around us, not in the spirit of political correctness, but rather in the spirit of biblical correctness. We need a multiethnic movement that exalts kingdom culture above all others and unifies us in its righteousness and justice.

We need to tear down the ethnic walls. We need to stop looking for slights and indulging in self-pity. We need to embrace those who we think fear us just as they need to embrace us. We need to remove those barriers and replace them with authentic Spirit-empowered bridges. We need a new pentecost in America.

The His-panic Factor

I'm often asked, "What is a Latino Christian? What do you believe? How would you describe your community?" The response is the summation of a simple recipe. A Latino evangelical is what you get when you take Billy Graham and Dr. Martin Luther King Jr., put them in a blender, and place salsa sauce on top.

This cross movement carries a definitive Hispanic flavor. Without a doubt, the force with the greatest potential to transform the narrative of twenty-first-century American evangelicalism is brown in color. As we hear again and again, our nation is currently undergoing a potentially transformative shift in its demographics. By midcentury, for the first time, America's population will be, as it pertains to ethnic composition, less than half "white."

Although often labeled "brown," Hispanics are not a race but rather an ethno-cultural group of various races coalescing around a common language and shared values. According to the 2010 census, the Hispanic population—at 16.39 percent of the US population—is the largest minority group in the country. With more than fifty million members now, this community has a future growth capacity unmatched by any other ethnic group. Roughly 75 percent of Hispanics are under forty years of age, and 34 percent are eighteen years of age or younger. By 2020, the Latino population will likely pass 100 million or 25 percent of the nation's population. The future of American Christianity, evangelicalism, and the next great harvest is in the Hispanic and immigrant community, and whether or not we reach out with compassion.

Unlike Europe, the bulk of whose immigrants come from a non-Christian culture often hostile to the host culture, America is blessed to have sympathetic Christian cultures south of our border. A study from Pew Research in 2007 concluded that 19 percent of Latinos identify themselves as Protestants, primarily evangelical, while 68 percent identify themselves as Catholics, 54 percent of them as Charismatic Catholics. In essence, close to 90 percent of all Hispanic Americans believe that Jesus died on the cross, rose from the dead, and is the eternal hope of glory for all mankind. This is a higher percentage than for the non-Hispanic population.[1]

We are part of a multiethnic church, rapidly becoming multilingual and committed to a kingdom culture presentation of the gospel. Hispanic evangelicals, in essence, represent the United Nations of Christianity. Hence, we must engage Latinos and others in order for the American church to truly reflect the church of Jesus Christ. We stand poised to change the Christian experience by broadening the evangelical agenda, incorporating a transformational missiology, reigniting a prophetic socio-political movement, and globally serving as ambassadors of a kingdom culture ethos that reconciles righteousness with justice.

How many Hispanics are allowed to come to America and stay here is the subject of an ongoing public policy debate in Washington and elsewhere. The debate has removed the burial clothes from an entire segment of our populace. It also provides an unprecedented opportunity for outreach and evangelism. The challenge is that agents other than Christians see an opportunity as well. Political parties are recruiting hard. The merchandisers are selling hard. Wall Street is exploiting hard. The multiculturalists are dividing hard. The separatists are radicalizing hard. Hollywood is corrupting hard. Christians are evangelizing, but not as hard as they should.

Not all signs are promising. The growth of the Hispanic community in America is compromised by the fact that roughly 53 percent of Hispanic babies are born out of wedlock. This percentage continues to increase as new immigrants yield to the so-called sexual revolution and the seduction of the welfare culture. This makes the work of the kingdom culture church all the more imperative. It is the only force that can compete with the material corruptions all Americans face.

If successful, the body of Christ stands ready to reap an Hispanic harvest, but it will not happen by itself. We have to transcend the historical perspective that the Hispanic population responds exclusively to ministries and churches in California, Texas, Florida, New York, and the Southwest. Today, Hispanics participate in communities from North Dakota to North Carolina; from Portland, Maine, to Portland, Oregon; from sea to shining sea. We will also need a clear and practical articulation of a biblical worldview, one based on the message of the cross.

Given the inevitability of change, any church or ministry committed to a viable twenty-first-century growth matrix must include an Hispanic outreach strategy. To stay relevant in ministry today, to carry out the Lamb's Agenda, evangelical leaders must reach out to Latinos. For the American church to continue to be viable, it must equip, train, collaborate with, and engage Hispanic American believers.

More importantly, I stand convinced that the Hispanic community's prophetic role lies defined in the very construct of the term Hispanic. First, it begins with *His*, capital *H*. Second, it continues with *panic*. His-panic, HISPANIC. Amigos, we are not here to teach America the Macarena, salsa, or the cha-cha-cha. We are not here to increase the dividend portfolios of those who have diversified by investing in Taco Bell. We are not here to make anyone press "1" for English or "2" for Spanish. We are here to bring panic to the kingdom of darkness in the name of Jesus Christ.

When history books write about twenty-first-century America, they will write about a new awakening, a Third Great Awakening, a modern revival. But this time the names will not be limited to Edwards, Wesley, or Whitefield. This time, the names will include García, Rivera, Miranda, Morales, and Sánchez. This community is quickly emerging as the most pro-life, pro-family, pro-biblical justice ethnic faith demographic in our nation. Hispanics maintain a commitment to a Christian worldview that carries sociopolitical implications. This is why Ronald Reagan affirmed the traditionalist thread embedded in the community and the mission "under God" central to Hispanic tradition. At the conclusion of his talk celebrating Hispanic Heritage Week in 1982 Reagan said:

> At the root of everything that we're trying to accomplish is the belief that America has a mission. We are a nation of freedom, living under God, believing all citizens must have the opportunity to grow, create wealth, and build a better life for those who follow. If we live up to those moral values, we can keep the American dream alive for our children and our grandchildren, and America will remain mankind's best hope. With your help, I know we can and we will. *Muchas gracias. Que Dios los bendiga.*

God bless you, too, President Reagan.

Immigrants and the Undocumented

In spite of the demographic shift, there exists some trepidation within Christian ministry concerning immigrant outreach. Some ask, "How do you reach out to a community that includes undocumented individuals? Are there legal ramifications or obligations as we render services to these individuals?"

First, the church carries a biblical imperative to reach out to every nation. Christ himself admonished us to make disciples of all people while simultaneously reminding us that we can only measure the viable execution of his Word in how we treat the most needy: "Truly I tell you, whatever you did for one of the least of these brothers and sisters of mine, you did for me" (Matthew 25:40).

We can trace biblical mandates to engage in compassionate evangelistic outreach to Leviticus 19:33–34: "When a foreigner resides among you in your land, do not mistreat them. The foreigner residing among you must be treated as your native-born. Love them as yourself, for you were foreigners in Egypt. I am the LORD your God."

Carlos Campo, president of Regent University, viewed this concern through the lens of the prophet Isaiah: "The undocumented are surely the poor wanderers of our day. Pastors have a moral duty to respond to them as they would any other brother or sister in need."[2] Albert Reyes, president of Buckner Services, believes that pastors and churches that reach out to the immigrant in essence deliver the same redemptive outreach exhibited by the Good Samaritan.[3]

The undocumented immigrant may represent the most alienated and rejected segment of our society—today's "least of these." Although a divisive issue, Bible-believing Americans have a moral and biblical responsibility to bring Jesus to the undocumented. Evangelicals and Christians committed to spreading the gospel must incorporate prophetic witness that heals communities, ushers in peace, and exalts righteousness and justice.

As we engage in compassion ministries, we must not allow the issues that fall under the purview of the federal government to distract us. Pastor Daniel DeLeón of Santa Ana, California, captured the spirit of outreach when he declared, "When I stand at the church to receive people, we don't ask them what their legal status is for we are concerned with the heart and not the card. In addition, we are not officers of the government; we are servants of the Lord."[4]

To that end, the kingdom metric of Christian witness lies within the rubric of doing justice, loving mercy, and walking humbly before God. Our mission is to fulfill the Great Commission, equip the saints, make disciples, and worship God in spirit and in truth. Let Uncle Sam enforce immigration laws while we embrace a church that reaches the lost for Christ.

RISK MANAGEMENT AND LIABILITIES

Here is a question that we often hear. If a church exercises the biblical mandate of reaching out to all people with compassion, including immigrants, can it suffer legal consequences if the individuals ministered to are undocumented?

The Department of Justice, the Attorney General's office, congressional representatives, White House officials, secular adjudicators, and ecclesiastical authorities all agree on one irrefutable fact: biblical ministry and outreach to immigrants, regardless of their status, carries no legal liability. Chief legal counsel to the National Hispanic Christian Leadership Conference, Everardo Zavala, explained:

> With the exception of deliberately employing undocumented
> individuals or transporting them across state lines, which does

construe a violation of the law, clergy are uniformly protected
by federal and state statutes throughout the United States.[5]

There are several principles churches should honor if they
are to reach immigrants successfully. The Hispanic Evangelical
Association and the Hispanic Mega Church Association have created a rubric of immigrant compassionate outreach. This includes
what all churches, especially rural and smaller size churches, need
to do to reach the immigrant community. The rubric includes
leadership engagement, symbiotic language-oriented programming, aesthetics, and community-building techniques.

For starters, compassion ministries must seek to build trust
with the immigrant community by removing cumbersome
documentation that may alienate the very community they intend
to serve. As the law protects legitimate outreach, church officials
need to minimize bureaucratic practices that alienate rather than
engage. For example, while certain food-distribution ministries
require registration, they ought not necessarily to require proof
of citizenship as part of that registration. The most effective,
immigrant-focused compassion ministries require minimal
disclosure of private information. Most require little or none.

When the American church understands that it carries
the spiritual and legal authority to assist the immigrant, the
church may emerge as the only trustworthy institution in the
community. Some immigrants are understandably anxious
about dealing with local, state, and federal agencies that assist
in food and needs-specific services. Many immigrants consider
the church the sole sanctuary for both spiritual and physical
needs. "If immigrants cannot trust the church, who can they
trust?" asks Mauricio Elizondo, a church planter with Hispanic
American Assemblies of God. He elaborated:

Many low-income Hispanic immigrant families avoid government agencies because they fear deportation. They work many hours in the fields and yet do not have enough to feed or provide for the basic needs of their families. We bear witness to the fact poverty, hunger, and despair have increased exponentially in the past few years in the immigrant community. With that reality we encounter an unfortunate simultaneous increase in many social ills such as addiction, domestic violence, teen pregnancy, and the proliferation of gang activity. The only hope is the church of Jesus Christ.[6]

Gilbert Vélez understands firsthand the dynamics of compassionate ministry. Vélez is senior pastor of the twenty-five-hundred-member Mercy Church, an Assemblies of God congregation in Laredo, Texas. Vélez also oversees the Hispanic Mega Church Association. "Compassion ministries must begin not just with services, goods, and outreach," stated Vélez. "But to effectively reach and engage the immigrant community, compassion ministries must build trust."[7]

Leadership Engagement

According to Vélez, "Any ministry committed to reaching the immigrant needs to employ personnel who speak the language and understand the cultural terrain."[8] Compassion outreach begins at the leadership level.

Churches committed to reaching the immigrant community must include ethnic and immigrant leadership in their governance. This will secure an institutionalized commitment, rather than a token or temporary effort. For example, if I want to plant a church and attract various ethnicities, church growth models indicate I will attract what I reflect in my leadership—from the praise and worship to the ushers and staff. My leadership team must reflect the community I desire to serve.

As Vélez observed, some within the immigrant community will view all non-ethnics, ministers included, as arms of the law. Faced with possible deportation and separation of families, they may avoid the very services that will heal their bodies and their spirits. To reassure these people, large churches will need bilingual ministers, and small churches will need bilingual volunteers.

It is not enough to speak the language of the community. The ministry must stand ready to teach the community the language of the church. We can help and should help immigrants speak English. They are hugely disadvantaged if they cannot. As one pastor in Texas said, "We will learn Spanish, and bring them to church where we provide English courses. The church can serve as the primary institution for both vertical integration into the Kingdom and horizontal integration into American society."[9]

AESTHETICS

Compassionate immigrant outreach requires an effort to communicate through the sensual symbols that reassure the community. This requires a simple cultural orientation to understand the basic threads embedded in the ethos of the community, from food to music to color schemes to iconography and other particularities. Cultural Orientation 101 can result in a great bounty.

Compassionate evangelistic outreach must also incorporate

messaging in both languages. Some ministries have a great spirit but lack the language-friendly resources to communicate effectively. For example, a primarily Anglo congregation in Dallas at the beginning of a school year targeted Hispanic families with school-age children. Church staffers rented a parking lot in the heart of the community, set up a truck, and brought in new backpacks stuffed with pencils, notebooks, calculators, and other school supplies.

Although the volunteers were in the right place at the right time doing the right thing, few families took advantage of the outreach. Why? Ministry organizers discovered after the event that all their advertising was in English. Effective, compassionate outreach to the Hispanic immigrant community requires both Spanish and English. In short, compassion and culture must intersect for effective evangelism to take place.

Community-building Techniques

Churches do well to shape ethnic and immigrant outreach by first understanding the role of the community in Hispanic culture. While American and Western European models celebrate the individual, Hispanic and immigrant groups tend to put more focus on community mobilization. "Celebrating culture and embracing the distinctive threads of our people can only lead to the mosaic we call the Kingdom," stated Jesse Miranda, executive presbyter of the Assemblies of God and chairman emeritus of the National Hispanic Evangelical Association. "We need ethnic outreach that begins in the head, moves to the hand, and finishes in the heart—the heart of the community."[10]

THE AGENDA OF THE LAMB

Compassion-based evangelism stems not from the narrative of a political ideology, but rather from the heart of prophetic witness. Reaching out to Hispanics and other immigrants—documented or otherwise—may not reflect the agenda of the Donkey or the Elephant, but it does reflect the Agenda of the Lamb. These immigrants, particularly Hispanic immigrants, have the potential to help reinforce America's Judeo-Christian heritage and restore our historic mission.

In essence, the Hispanic immigrant demonstrates affinity with the core values that permeate the American Bible-believing, Spirit-filled church—commitment to biblical orthodoxy, holiness, and the power of the Holy Spirit. With God's blessing and our help, immigrant Christians will emerge in the twenty-first century as the firewall of righteousness and justice against spiritual apathy, moral relativism, and cultural decay.

Compassionate outreach may very well serve as the balm of Gilead in healing the current strife between native and immigrant. God willing, it will result not only in the salvation of the immigrant community, but also in the salvation of the American church.

THE PETER AND JOHN MOVEMENT

Twentieth-century Christian movements do not necessarily work in the twenty-first century. For example, while the Moral Majority of Jerry Falwell and the Christian Coalition of Pat Robertson called biblical voters to engage in political activity after decades of apathy, the membership composition spoke to a constituency that was too male, too old, and too white to be sustainable.

Furthermore, in a world of social networking—Facebook, Twitter, iPads, and YouTube—only a multiethnic kingdom culture movement can succeed in executing the Lamb's Agenda. As a model, the response to Proposition 8 in California represents a working collaborative kingdom model for others to emulate.

This was the proposition that served to affirm the historical definition of marriage between one man and one woman. To the surprise of many, the two demographic segments of the state that voted in significant majorities to preserve the biblical definition of marriage were the African Americans and the Hispanics. Seventy percent of black voters and 53 percent of Hispanic voters voted to preserve marriage. Together, they pulled the total statewide numbers to 52 percent, a bare majority.[11]

What makes these numbers even more impressive is that black and Hispanic voters had to buck the political pressures from the party with which most of them align and shut out the media pressure from a scolding entertainment industry.

This kind of alliance can happen again. These two communities stand poised to activate an impermeable kingdom culture, a multiethnic firewall in defense of life, family, and religious liberty. They have their resolve already.

Despite the accusations from Proposition 8 opponents, this was not about homophobia. No serious Christian would treat a homosexual with anything but respect and dignity. We know how Jesus responded to all members of society regardless of how others expected him to respond. John 8:1–7 famously tells us of Jesus' visit to the temple courts, where all the people gathered around him, and he proceeded to teach them. Hoping to trap Jesus, the teachers of the law and the Pharisees brought in an accused woman and said, "Teacher, this woman was caught in the act of adultery. In the Law Moses commanded us to stone such women. Now what do you say?"

Jesus confused them by writing on the ground with his finger while they talked. When his inquisitors kept on questioning him, Jesus stood up and said, "Let any one of you who is without sin be the first to throw a stone at her." This is not to say that Jesus approved of her behavior—he did not—but he recognized that she was worthy of mercy and understanding.

No, what the supporters of Proposition 8 were saying to the larger accusatory culture was that marriage mattered. It cannot be redefined to fit current fashions. Historically, the federal government has fought to protect traditional marriage. In its 1856 platform, for instance, the Republican Party vowed "to prohibit in the territories those twin relics of barbarism: polygamy and slavery." The following year, Democratic president James Buchanan sent federal troops to Utah to end the practice of polygamy and to protect traditional marriage. This had nothing to do with homosexuality.

Many Americans, including the majority of African Americans and Hispanics, recognize the need to preserve marriage as the primary antidote to teen pregnancy, violence, crime, gang activity, and other social ills. I refer here to a marriage where mom *and* dad are present. In California, black and Hispanic voters served as something of an ethnic firewall so that the media could not easily caricature angry white evangelicals as the source of all their problems.

In addition to a solid commitment to vertical truth, Hispanics and African Americans face horizontal justice challenges in the nation's urban centers. Not coincidentally, many of these flow from the breakdown in marriage. More than 70 percent of African American babies are born out of wedlock across all classes. The rate among Hispanics has passed 50 percent and continues to climb as new immigrants adapt to the seductions of the culture and the inducements of a welfare system that unthinkingly rewards only those family households without a father present.

"Where the marriage culture begins to erode," argues the Manhattan Declaration, "social pathologies of every sort quickly manifest themselves." If fatherless homes are a problem, fatherless neighborhoods are a nightmare. Unsupervised, boys will find all the trouble that a free society offers. This includes drugs, crime, gangs, and a general withdrawal from ordered society. The poorest and most vulnerable among us, states the Manhattan Declaration, are "paying a huge price in delinquency, drug abuse, crime, incarceration, hopelessness, and despair."[12]

African Americans have a high school drop out rate nearly twice that of whites, and Hispanics nearly twice that of blacks. Those minorities who do attend high school are often thrown together in volatile urban environments where blacks and Hispanics are encouraged to see each other as enemies. In prisons, the tension between ethnic groups hovers at orange alert levels.

Only an awakening, a Third Great Awakening, has the potential to transform anger into alliance, conflict into cooperation, futility into fruitfulness. For with the cross, and in the kingdom culture spirit of pentecost, Hispanics, African Americans, Asian Americans, Native Americans, European Americans, and all of God's children—American and otherwise—approach the proverbial gate called Beautiful.

Before us lies a crippled and paralyzed world begging for substance, begging for change, begging for hope. And from the

8.

AN HD OR ANALOG MOVEMENT

AS OF FEBRUARY 2009, THROUGHOUT AMERICA all televisions began receiving their signals exclusively by way of a digital format rather than through the traditional analog format. Today, to watch your favorite television program, *Dancing with the Stars* or *American Idol* or *NCIS*, you must either have a high-definition TV or an apparatus that makes your television HD compatible. The government described this historic transition as "the end of the rabbit ears."

To fulfill the Agenda of the Lamb, the American church must move out of its own "rabbit ears" era. The choice, today, is to make the necessary modifications or to appear as obsolete as an analog TV. Unfortunately, the signal the American church now sends about who God is and what he is saying comes across broken and blurry, especially to the so-called "Millennials" (those born after 1980).

For too many people today of all age groups, even those who are affiliated with a church, Sunday morning is little more than a social occasion, an opportunity to dress up, visit with friends, listen to an idle hour of feel-good preaching and singing, and go to brunch afterward, utterly unmoved about changing one's life.

To make matters worse, scandals fill pulpits, divorces destroy families, and our youth embrace an empty universalism while we preach more about money than we do about the soul. This is rabbit-ears Christianity, nothing more or less than a church transmitting fuzzy signals to a dwindling audience.

Just as HDTV enhances the quality of televised images exponentially, so, too, do we need to transmit a high-definition picture of a gospel that is both incarnating and transforming. What does an HD church look like? Let's not forget high definition is about image resolution, clarity of picture, speed of information, and multi-faceted engagement through on-demand programming, Internet transmission, and networking. Thus, an HD church will present a clear picture of a loving God who repudiates sin while loving the sinner.

Without a doubt, a fresh holiness movement needs to take place, with a commitment to addressing a sin-tolerant culture but without the vestiges of legalism. This church will incorporate the eternal truth, "I am the LORD your God; consecrate yourselves and be holy, because I am holy" (Lev. 11:44).

Second, an HD Lamb's Agenda movement in America will require engagement and interaction with the culture. However, American culture cannot merely be engaged by the church. It must be reformed through the church. We need a clear picture, a biblical and righteous transmission of God, family, morality, righteousness, and justice to compete with the relentlessly violent and hedonistic imagery that is now subverting our youth.

Thirdly, high-definition Christianity in America requires programs, systems, institutions, delivery mechanisms, and finally, communities that can facilitate clear and viable transmission of the gospel. Yes, high-definition enables television viewers to multitask, work on the Internet, order on demand, and entertain. But Christianity has much more to offer than even the best home entertainment center. The church can address the social, spiritual, physical, intellectual, and communal needs of all its constituents. To do so, it can no longer try to compete as "entertainment." It must go deeper and reach higher. It must reconcile the vertical with horizontal planes of the cross. And it must have the means of conveying the cross's message.

Churches that upgrade and modernize their tools of transmission will be relevant in the twenty-first-century American religious scene. And by "tools" I do not necessarily mean bigger TV screens or better sound systems. I mean spiritual tools. Our nation needs an *ecclesia* (church) that embodies *habitus Christus* (the life and habits of Christ) with a clear signal that transmits an *imago Dei* (image of God) who still saves, delivers, heals, and will return. Goodbye rabbit ears, welcome awakening!

Upgrade to a Multigenerational Platform

Upgrading to an HD Lamb's Agenda delivery system requires serious rethinking. Why? American Christianity stands at the edge of a spiritual abyss. Either we vault across it to a new promised land on the other side or we descend into the depths of quasi-spiritual, European-style irrelevance. To make this prophetic leap, and to sustain its promise, the church in America must display its implicit strength and transfer that spiritual DNA to the next generation.

Surveys tell us that young people today are not fully tuned

in. A comprehensive Pew survey from 2010 showed some areas of concern and some areas of promise. On the concern side, nearly 25 percent of Millennials claimed no religious affiliation. Not only was this higher than other age group, but this number is also higher than it was for baby boomers or Generation Xers at the same stage of their lives. These young adults also attended religious services less often than older Americans, and fewer young people said that religion was very important in their lives.

Also of concern, only 68 percent of Americans aged eighteen to twenty-nine identified as Christians, compared to 81 percent of Americans over thirty. Similarly, young adults were less convinced of God's existence than their elders were. Only 64 percent of Millennials claimed to be absolutely certain of God's existence, compared with 73 percent of those thirty and older.

On the promise side, Millennials were just as likely as those over thirty to believe in life after death, heaven, hell, and miracles. On several of these variables, young mainline Protestants and congregants at historically black churches showed higher levels of belief than their elders. Among Protestants, both evangelical and mainline, those eighteen- to twenty-nine-year-olds affiliated with a church were more likely to see theirs as the one true faith than their seniors. And although there are some differences on specific social issues, those under thirty were just as likely to believe in absolute standards of right and wrong as those over thirty.[1]

In short, America remains a deeply Christian and thoroughly spiritual country. If not yet in the hearts of the young, Christ is still in the air, and young people sense it. I see the lack of affiliation among them as more of an opportunity than a problem. We know they cry out for something to believe in, a spiritual connection, a depth of feeling and believing that their lives currently lack.

In the hours before her death, as her life spun fatally out

of control, pop star Whitney Houston was quoting Bible passages and crying out for Jesus. The day before she was found in the bath of her Los Angeles hotel, Houston told one friend, "I'm gonna go see Jesus. I want to see Jesus." The next day, with her death imminent, she was reported to have said, "You know, he's so cool. I really want to see that Jesus."[2] A cruel popular culture could kill Houston, but it could not kill her faith. What she needed, however, was more than a memory of Jesus. She needed his presence in her life. All of us do, young and old.

Like Houston, too many Americans search but don't find. They fail to connect Abraham, Isaac, and Jacob. One recent study revealed that 25 percent of all adults abandoned their childhood faith while 44 percent changed religious affiliation. These numbers raise the question: Should Christians be concerned with rejection and drift, and should their respective communities position themselves for next-generation relevancy?

First, we must come to the full recognition that in America we tend to measure inheritance and heritage obligations within the rubric of materialism. We fret about wealth management, estate taxes, and transmission schemes, but we rarely worry about dying spiritually intestate. And yet our greatest potential gift to our children and their children flows from our faith. The best asset we can ever leave behind is not an estate or a trust fund but rather the powerful truth embodied in a simple phrase, "as for me and my household, we will serve the Lord" (Joshua 24:15).

To build for the future, successful churches and ministries must also learn to build a platform on which Abraham's faith converges with Isaac's passion and Jacob's tenacity. In other words, leaders must create and implement strategies that connect the generations through a commonality of purpose rather than a pandering to generational differences.

Many church leaders sift through a wide variety of available strategies to reach the various generations. Although the exponential increase in the style of contemporary worship services—illustrated sermons, digital Christianity, etc.—speaks to the reality of customization, any outreach advantage comes to naught if the medium obscures the message. Marshall McLuhan famously said "the medium is the message," but that is only true in Christianity if we understand the medium to be Jesus Christ.

Nearly two centuries ago, Barton W. Stone, one of the leaders of the Second Great Awakening, made much the same point that I am making here:

> I suggest we restore the church as it was in the New Testament day, rooting it firmly in the pattern set by the early disciples. With its roots there, it can sway and bend to adjust to the times, but fundamentally it would always be the same. A strong tree is still a tree whatever winds blow. And the church would still be the church despite men's opinions blowing about it.[3]

Not only must we connect Abraham, Isaac, and Jacob through the delivery platforms of services and ministries offered at the local church, but we must also connect the generations through the bridge of a reconciled narrative. There now exists a generational disconnect as well as a biblical disconnect. We connected the previous generations with the Word. Young people have lost this connection. Their lack of biblical literacy makes the transmission of our Christian heritage difficult no matter how modern a church's audiovisuals. The Word will connect our generations and serve as the catalyst for American Christianity for years to come.

Simply stated, the Abrahams of our lifetime have stood on

the Word, the Isaacs have thrived on worship, and the Jacobs have cried out for justice. Can we be a church that addresses the spiritual distinctions of all three and that emerges as the nexus of biblical orthodoxy, holiness, worship, and justice? Can we rise with the dictum of the Nicene Creed while we worship in spirit and truth, all the while drafting a narrative of justice?

While advancing the Lamb's Agenda, kingdom culture Christians who bridge the generations will cry out in the midst of moral relativism, cultural terrorism, and spiritual despair, "God of Abraham, Isaac, and Jacob." Then, the God who provided the ram, the wells, and the ladder will provide the same for our generation and for the generations yet to come.

A 3-D Movement

Yet, we cannot stop with high-definition. The current trend in visual delivery and video imaging dissemination attempts to capture the breadth and depth of our senses—3-D technology. While depth perception extends to media beyond the normative entertainment alternatives, the Lamb's Agenda requires a 3-D visual where the vertical and horizontal serve as the primary delivery mechanism for the depth of the way, the truth, and the life. Our movement must be three dimensional. The Lamb's Agenda brings depth of clarity and perception to the narrow way, the uncompromised truth, and the abundant life.

In America today there are any number of paths to moral relativism, spiritual apathy, and cultural decay. There are far too many. But there is, of course, another path. Jesus said, "I am the way, the truth, and the life." Let me be clear. Although what I am about to say is not politically correct, and although it runs counter to the standard modus operandi of the moment, it must be said: There is only one—yes, *one*—way to God and heaven. Jesus is the Way, the narrow way, the only way. The Lamb's Agenda provides a clear direction. To a world obsessed with global positioning systems for assistance, it proposes a direct route to vertical salvation and horizontal transformation, the Lamb's route.

Furthermore, a 3-D Lamb's Agenda movement melds truth with love. We need Christian leadership that breaks through the vestiges of religiosity and lukewarm Christianity with biblical truth. My friends, truth is not subject to the cultural proclivities of the moment. Truth comes not from media pundits on CNN, Fox News, MSNBC, ABC, NBC, CBS, talk radio, bloggers, and publications with their secular agendas and slanted reporting. Oh, and by the way, neither is there such a thing as white truth, black truth, or brown truth. There is one eternal truth: Jesus is the Truth. As we learn in John 8:32, "Then you will know the truth, and the truth will set you free."

I understand. Everything seems to be changing. I understand that this is the age of Twitter, Facebook, e-mail, digital platforms, optics, metrics, rubrics, and constant change. But there is one thing that never changes: "Jesus Christ is the same yesterday and today and forever" (Hebrews 13:8). This idea is reinforced in Matthew 24:35: "Heaven and earth will pass away, but my words will never pass away." In the midst of a changing world there exists truth that never changes. The Lamb's Agenda requires an uncompromised commitment to that biblical truth.

Although we walk on this narrow way of truth, we experience life, and we experience it abundantly. You see, Jesus came to give us life, and he gave us life in abundance.

9.

JOHN THE BAPTIST LEADERSHIP

MOVEMENTS STAND OR FALL BASED ON ONE significant element: leadership. While the movement depends on its messaging and mobilization platforms to establish itself, long-term sustainability demands quality leadership, and quality leadership does not happen by accident.

The Agenda of the Lamb movement will require many voices and many leaders. The question arises: What leadership style can best reconcile the vertical and horizontal planes of the cross? The answer is embodied in the person Christ himself recognized as a leader extraordinaire—John the Baptist.

In this context, it is important to understand that any worthwhile, large-scale, human endeavor begins with an overarching philosophical vision. This vision provides the theoretical framework within which an individual can pose questions, address concrete situations, and make crucial decisions.

Thus, our larger metaphysical vision, in which all human actions are understood and rendered meaningful, dictates the theoretical paradigm we employ as leaders. The John the Baptist leadership model is an unusual paradigm. Most leadership models define success in the here and now, and many leaders seek to be acknowledged, if not rewarded, for the success they achieve.

THE JOHN THE BAPTIST MODEL

By contrast, the John the Baptist model is that rare paradigm in which leaders measure success by how they have helped their followers become even better leaders than they themselves are. However rare the use of this model, it is the one that creates all the world's great and lasting movements, none greater or more lasting than the movement we call the Agenda of the Lamb. Leaders who are willing to prepare the way, baptize their successors, and finally conclude tenure by handing over to their appointed heirs the metaphorical gavel will in the end assure consistency and continuity.

Cross leadership demands commitment and virtue. The very notion of the cross—vertical and horizontal—requires a leader capable of understanding and explaining its meaning. Successful leadership helps create an environment in which movements, institutions, corporations, and communities thrive by reconciling the *imago Dei* with the *habitus Christi*.

The immediate directive of cross leadership is to enrich, enhance, and empower the movement by providing the intellectual wherewithal, spiritual fortitude, and business acumen necessary for success. The long-term directive is to secure the continuity of success by amplifying other voices and making those who follow greater than oneself.

The very notion of making succession a priority, even from

the start of a leader's tenure, demands an abandonment of ego. Cross leadership is not about fashioning a movement that hinges on one individual. It is not about identifying the movement with any one person. It is ultimately about Jesus Christ, and any name that looms larger on the marquee outside the church undermines the movement. Besides, an ego-centered movement rarely has a life expectancy beyond the person who launches it.

Cross leadership demands humility, deference, and respect for the movement. It obligates leaders to create a succession plan founded in integrity and accountability. More practically, that plan should factor in a corporate affinity for discipleship building and a contractual obligation for sustaining excellence.

THE MOSES PRECURSOR

By way of example, consider Moses as we meet him in the Old Testament. Much in the way John the Baptist prepared the way for Jesus, Moses prepared the way for Joshua. In spite of personal failures that denied him any meaningful entry into the land of promise, Moses made sure that Joshua was prepared to succeed him after he died. This is a point that the Lord himself made in anointing Joshua as Moses' successor.

"Be strong and very courageous," the Lord told Joshua. "Be careful to obey all the law my servant Moses gave you; do not turn from it to the right or to the left, that you may be successful wherever you go" (Joshua 1:7). Moses prepared a leader who would take his people farther than he ever could. This is what good leaders do.

Moses groomed his successor from within his own people. This is a good practice for any church, movement, or community.

Leadership boards may want to reconsider the policy of looking outside for succession. Enduring movements do not recruit leaders. They develop leaders from within. Jim Collins, the leadership guru, confirms this very point. His research on successful companies showed an undeniable pattern: companies that make the leap from good to great seek out and appoint successors who have been groomed within the organization.

Joshua did not plan for succession as wisely or as carefully as Moses. His lack of deliberation within his leadership domain resulted in Israel's chaotic and inconsistent history after his death. We have seen this problem in our nation's own history. Abraham Lincoln's assassination left his movement in the hands of Andrew Johnson, who was unprepared to sustain it. Instead of a nation united after the Civil War, we had to struggle through a century of Jim Crow and a subsequent half-century of racial unease.

The man who had the potential to address that unease and move the nation forward, Martin Luther King Jr., was unable to groom a successor with anywhere near his own combination of character and charisma. Those with the charisma lacked the character. Those with the character lacked the charisma. King's assassination, like Lincoln's, left the preparation process incomplete. To a large degree, his movement lost direction after his death.

THE JESUS EXAMPLE

Jesus established a leadership model that cannot truly be followed. Nevertheless, that model tells us a good deal about the value he placed on succession and continuity. "And I tell you that you are Peter, and on this rock I will build my church, and the gates of Hades will not overcome it," Jesus told us in Matthew 16:18–19. "I will give you the keys of the kingdom of heaven; whatever you bind on earth will be bound in heaven, and whatever you loose on earth will be loosed in heaven."

In the days following his resurrection, Jesus reinforced Peter's authority and prepared his apostles for their mission going forward, a preparation that culminated at pentecost. Significantly, it was Peter who addressed the perplexed crowds after the event. After reassuring them that the apostles were not drunk, that they were filled instead with the Holy Spirit, Peter told the crowds what was expected of them:

Repent and be baptized, every one of you, in the name of Jesus Christ for the forgiveness of your sins. And you will receive the gift of the Holy Spirit. The promise is for you and your children and for all who are far off—for all whom the Lord our God will call. (Acts 2:38–39)

One can forgive the skeptics in that crowd—and there were more than a few—for thinking that this movement would not last out the year. Two thousand years later, the more than two billion Christians in the world prove the skeptics seriously wrong. What is impressive is that what Peter believed that day about Jesus—that he died on the cross and rose again from the dead to forgive us our sins—we still believe firmly today. Despite various schisms, dissents, and imperfect shepherding, the church has remained remarkably constant over those two millennia. No ordinary mortal could have prepared a movement that thoroughly, but as a model it has much to admire and emulate.

ENDURING PILLARS

Successful movement leadership begins with an understanding of the requirements of enduring leadership as exemplified by John the Baptist. These recommendations might best be thought of as the pillars of cross leadership, pillars upon which sustained success can be based. Let us begin with the first pillar, preparation:

> In those days John the Baptist came, preaching in the wilderness of Judea and saying, "Repent, for the kingdom of heaven has come near." This is he who was spoken of through the prophet Isaiah:
>
> "A voice of one calling in the wilderness,
>   'Prepare the way for the Lord,
>   make straight paths for him.'" (Matthew 3:1–3)

No other phrase defines the leadership tenure of John the Baptist better than this, "Prepare the way for the Lord!" The deafening call of one proven leader on another's behalf resonated throughout the hills and valleys of Israel. John the Baptist existed for this one great purpose: to prepare the way for the Christ. To do this, he had to sublimate his own ego and assume a secondary role, and he did so gladly.

In personal leadership development, we all experience a John the Baptist season right before our Jesus season. Preparation always precedes revelation. A vertical and horizontal leadership motif comes with the built-in responsibility to prepare the way for our successor.

This kind of prophetic outlook does not limit the current leader to a lame-duck status. Quite the contrary is true. Preparing the way avoids unexpected leadership issues. Preparing the way leverages the current resources for tomorrow's success. Preparing the way includes mentorship, personal accountability, and the careful transference of spiritual, intellectual, and organizational capital.

As happens all too often today, inside and outside of the church, the departure of a leader results in a generalized atrophy of ideas, vision, and technical expertise. It is different for John the Baptist leaders. They do not see their talents as portable. Those talents belong to the movement or, as John the Baptist would say, to "the kingdom."

These leaders know they must invest their own human capital in the church and in the leadership that will succeed them. These leaders prepare for transition not through some cold bureaucratic structure but by developing and cultivating relationships with potential successors. The Lamb's Agenda depends on leaders capable of honoring those relationships.

Remembering Who the Messiah Is

Unfortunately, the phrase "messianic complex" describes too many people in leadership positions today. They may not say it out loud, but they think of themselves as a messiah or something very close to it. John the Baptist leaders know otherwise. They know they are not anyone's saviors. They know they are preparing the way for what follows. They know that a multi-tiered progression of disciplined achievements is what builds a future.

"Repent, for the kingdom of heaven has come near," said John the Baptist. He did not shy away from his essential marketing task, announcing the virtues of the movement from its very inception. He had mastered emotional branding long before today's experts like Marc Gobé coined the term. Jesus was not another prophet. He was "the Lord," the one who could return joy to the world, and John was proud to introduce him.

Today, John the Baptist leaders specialize in being the oracles of a movement's destiny. They do not take credit for the movement's success. Rather, they affirm those whom they have followed, thank those who have helped them, and, more importantly, prepare for those who are still to come.

John the Baptist leaders understand that preparing the way takes work. What they do today matters, as their success will help prepare the field for the righteousness and justice movement to come. They must be able to identify the possible obstacles to future success, address them, confront them, overcome them, and leave a clear field for their successors.

Preparation at times demands confrontation. A classic biblical example illustrates this point. Confronted with various plagues and judgments from God, a stubborn Pharaoh refused to grant liberty to the Hebrew children. God hardened his heart: "At midnight the LORD struck down all the firstborn in Egypt, from the firstborn of Pharaoh, who sat on the throne, to the firstborn of the prisoner, who was in the dungeon, and the firstborn of all the livestock as well" (Exodus 12:29).

God waited for Pharaoh's son to die in order to release the Hebrew children. Why? God was not looking at the present but rather he looked into the future and removed a potential enemy to the children of Israel. He also set a precedent for justice that would ring down through the ages: "Go down, Moses/ Way down in Egypt's land/ Tell old Pharaoh/ To let My people go!"[1]

Then and now, prophetic leadership carries the responsibility of removing obstacles and potential threats to the success and viability of the movement—not just in the present, but also for the foreseeable future. This leadership should be grounded in relationships. It should "brand" the greater vision in a respectful way. It should proudly trumpet the fulfillment of that vision, and it should confront the forces that would block that fulfillment.

BAPTISM BY WATER

Like John the Baptist, twenty-first-century prophetic leaders distinguish themselves by submerging leaders and followers in water, not fire.

> The next day John saw Jesus coming toward him and said, "Look, the Lamb of God, who takes away the sin of the world! This is the one I meant when I said, 'A man who comes after me has surpassed me because he was before me.' I myself did not know him, but the reason I came baptizing with water was that he might be revealed to Israel."
>
> Then John gave this testimony: "I saw the Spirit come down from heaven as a dove and remain on him. And I myself did not know him, but the one who sent me to baptize with water told me, 'The man on whom you see the Spirit come down and remain is the one who will baptize with the Holy Spirit.' " (John 1:29–33)

John's declaration, along with God's affirmation, transformed this ordinary ritual into an extraordinary opportunity to proclaim something new and better to come. There is a lesson here. John the Baptist leaders can achieve greater success by publicly articulating the mission, branding the movement, continually refreshing the vision, and evoking physical and verbal affirmation. A John the Baptist leader enjoys baptizing others into leadership. He knows that successors require full immersion in the ethos, vision, and purpose of the movement.

A John the Baptist leader also knows the limits of his mission. As it becomes clear in Matthew 3:11, John the Baptist certainly did. "I baptize you with water for repentance. But after me comes one who is more powerful than I, whose sandals I am not worthy to carry. He will baptize you with the Holy Spirit and fire." As John the Baptist leaders, it is not our role to baptize successors or potential successors in fire. Our role is limited to water. Time, character, and development will intrinsically execute the fire baptism.

Moreover, Matthew's gospel states that after being baptized Jesus rose up immediately from the waters and beheld the heavens were open. "And he saw the Spirit of God descending like a dove and alighting on him. And a voice from heaven said, 'This is my Son, whom I love; with him I am well pleased'" (3:16–17).

This historic baptism reveals a good deal about the nature of Lamb's Agenda leadership. Properly interpreted, it requires that men and women be willing to immerse followers in the waters of the movement, but they must be equally willing to release those followers to rise and ascend. Prophetic leaders do not fear the elevation of those around them. They welcome it.

Notice how John did not drown Jesus with bureaucratic trivia, did not try to dominate him, did not presume to be the center of attention, but rather he focused all attention on Christ. At the right time, Christ rose up out of the waters, saw the heavens open, and heard a voice. It is powerful validation like this that enables a movement to capture souls and conquer the world.

Although obviously not on this scale, John the Baptist

leaders experience physical and verbal affirmations as well. Such affirmations are hard to define and harder to predict, but they happen. And when they do, as leadership expert and historian Donald T. Phillips discovered, leaders sense a renewed power to motivate followers and complete initiatives.

THE ULTIMATE SACRIFICE

Finally, John the Baptist leaders must be willing to pay the ultimate sacrifice for the sake of the movement. John certainly did. Despite threats to his safety, he stuck to his principles and reminded Herod that he could not marry his brother's wife, Herodias. She plotted revenge and got it: "So he immediately sent an executioner with orders to bring John's head. The man went, beheaded John in the prison, and brought back his head on a platter" (Mark 6:27–28).

John's head was notoriously placed on a platter for public display. Although, happily, this is not the way most movement leaders end their day, John's public death holds a message for us nonetheless. He had by this time cleared the way for his successor and had been very open about it. There would be no schism following his death, no divided loyalties, no striving for succession.

After John's death, "the apostles gathered around Jesus and reported to him all they had done and taught" (Mark 6:30). They knew what to do and where to go. The movement would carry on with greater force than ever.

Placing the head on the platter is more about closure than death. It defines the character of a leader more vividly than any public acknowledgement or accolade. A leader who is willing to remove him- or herself—or be removed—for the sake of launching another embodies the twenty-first-century paradigm for a movement's success. This success demands leadership that prepares the way, that baptizes others in water, and that forsakes personal ambitions for the sake of the movement. Such leaders secure success in leadership transference as movements go from glory to glory.

10.

RECONCILING THE VERTICAL LAMB WITH THE HORIZONTAL LION

ONE AFTERNOON, I HAPPENED TO CATCH A television special on the subject of lions. The camera showed a lion in his natural habitat. He had just come back from a hunt with enough meat to feed his pride. As he stood and watched the lioness and cubs eat, he stared into the evening sky contemplating that next meal. Soon enough, he wandered off again into the savanna and returned, according to the narrator, "brutally and mortally wounded."

The lion has one real enemy in the animal world, namely other lions, rival lions that want what he has. In captivity, male lions often live more than twenty years. In the wild, they are lucky to live as long as ten. The wild is a brutal place. In this case, as the footage revealed, his rivals had ambushed our protagonist. He barely managed to return to his camp, scarred and bleeding. "Here we have the lion. The proud king of the jungle now stands wounded without strength to raise his head, lift up his paws and claws, or even open up his eyes," said the narrator.[1]

Amidst his "pride"—an apt name for the cubs and lionesses who depended on him—the wounded lion sat waiting for the inevitable. With a sense of triumph the same enemies that ambushed the lion returned to serve a final blow. As the enemies drew closer and began their assault, the same wounded lion that could not raise his head or lift his paws suddenly breathed a sound. It seemed faint at first, but it surged and turned into a savage snarl and then a full-throated roar of the sort that nightmares are made of.

With some accuracy, Proverbs 30:30 describes the lion as "mighty among beasts, who retreats before nothing." Immediately and without exception, the startled enemies of this lion fled into the wilderness leaving the cubs unharmed and food uneaten. The narrator captured it best when he said, "The enemies of the lion know very well that as long as the lion can roar, they cannot take away what belongs to him!"

There are times when a Christian, too, must be a lion. Yet, as much we might admire them, we cannot be like the lions in the wild. We have a double obligation. We are called upon to defend the cross's horizontal plane with, when necessary, a lion's roar. And yet, at the same time, we are asked to embrace the metaphorical motif embodied in the simplicity of the lamb—humility, gentleness, and submission.

The lambs and the sheep know the Shepherd's voice. As such, we stand vertically with great humility and submission as the Good Shepherd guides us through the pastures of life. So much a part of our collective heritage is this metaphor that even non-Christians can quote Psalm 23, here translated in the classic King James language:

The LORD is my shepherd; I shall not want.
He maketh me to lie down in green pastures: he leadeth me

beside the still waters.

*He restoreth my soul: he leadeth me in the paths of righteous-
ness for his name's sake.*

*Yea, though I walk through the valley of the shadow of
death, I will fear no evil: for thou art with me; thy rod and
thy staff they comfort me.*

*Thou preparest a table before me in the presence of mine ene-
mies: thou anointest my head with oil; my cup runneth over.*

*Surely goodness and mercy shall follow me all the days of
my life: and I will dwell in the house of the* LORD *for ever.*

Jesus Christ, of course, fulfilled the promise of the psalms.
"I am the good shepherd; I know my sheep and my sheep know
me," we learn in John 10:14–15. "Just as the Father knows me
and I know the Father—and I lay down my life for the sheep."

As Christians, we are finally both lions and lambs, horizontal lions and vertical lambs. As lambs, we maintain a vertical
silence of reverence and humility. We are not afraid to kneel, to
submit ourselves to God's mercy, to lie down in his green pastures. As lions, let loose in a world of rival lions more savage than
we can ever be, we nonetheless have an imperative to roar when
enemies of our faith threaten our offspring and our culture.

As lions, our responsibility is broad. "I have other sheep
that are not of this sheep pen," said the Good Shepherd. "I must
bring them also. They too will listen to my voice, and there shall
be one flock and one shepherd" (John 10:16). No one anywhere,
no matter what the nationality or the faith, is beyond our concern. The world is our pride.

For many secular activists, roaring is easy enough. Say whatever comes to mind as loudly as you can say it and follow up
with violence if it seems to help your cause. After all, in a world

without God, as Fyodor Dostoyevsky famously said, "Everything is permitted."

For a Christian, everything is not permitted. Our role as lion is tempered by our relationship with Christ. We have to ask ourselves at critical moments, "What would Jesus do?" We cannot forget our humility before God, our adherence to his law, and our commitment to the truth. Our roar cannot be one of confrontation and instigation, but must be one of revelation and reconciliation.

Our roar must prompt the serpent, the wolf, and the fox to flee, but it must also shower them with truth and love, however unwanted. Our roar must convey a message that Christianity and the transformative message of righteousness and justice will never be silenced. Finally, our roar must clearly present the imagery of the One who was crucified a lamb and resurrected a lion. It is not at all easy to convey this kind of information and still roar, but roar we must.

THE VERTICAL ALIGNMENT

Some Christians prefer to roar vertically and remain passive horizontally. Indeed, more than a few pastors encourage their congregants to yell at God, express their anger, and demand that he keep the promises that the congregant presumes he made.

One finds a particularly loud vertical roar among those who have abandoned—or are trying to abandon—their faith. Catholic author Flannery O'Connor captures this phenomenon in her classic 1952 novel *Wise Blood*. Hazel Motes, the novel's embittered protagonist, set out to prove his new-found atheism by creating "a Church Without Christ," a church without God for that matter; a church where, in O'Connor's words, "there was no Fall because there was nothing to fall from and no redemption because there was no Fall and no Judgment because there wasn't the first two."[2] In attempting to deny Christ as violently and publicly as he could, Motes came to see that there is no escaping the pull of God's grace.

One finds some useful words of wisdom on this larger subject in James 1:12: "Blessed is the one who perseveres under trial because, having stood the test, that person will receive the crown of life that the Lord has promised to those who love him."

We all face trials. For the Christian lamb, with a proper understanding of his or her vertical alignment with God, trials present opportunities to grow in God's grace and in our own character. "When tempted, no one should say, 'God is tempting me,'" James continues. "For God cannot be tempted by evil, nor does he tempt anyone; but each person is tempted when they are dragged away by their own evil desire and enticed" (James 1:13).

Anger is rarely a useful emotion, and anger at God is particularly unwarranted. James said, "My dear brothers and sisters, take note of this: Everyone should be quick to listen, slow to speak and slow to become angry, because human anger does not produce the righteousness that God desires" (James 1:19–20).

THE HORIZONTAL ROAR

Lions feature heavily in Christian tradition. There are many references to lions in the Old Testament, and all of them suggest the relative power that the lion possesses. Although the lions spared Daniel—"My God sent his angel, and he shut the mouths of the lions. They have not hurt me, because I was found innocent in his sight" (Daniel 6:22)—they are almost always seen as "the other," the amoral, external force that threatens and destroys God's sheep.

As we are reminded in Jeremiah 50:17, "Israel is a scattered flock that lions have chased away. The first to devour them was the king of Assyria; the last to crush their bones was Nebuchadnezzar king of Babylon." In Christianity's early centuries, of course, lions were more than metaphorical. To satisfy pagan gods and stimulate local passions, Christians were periodically fed to very real lions.

That did not stop the early Christians. Indeed, their faith and fortitude in the face of death inspired others. Within a few hundred years after Christ's resurrection, Christianity would become the dominant religion in the land and would outlast the Roman Empire by some fifteen centuries—and still counting.

In some countries today, Christians are treated no better than they were in the early days of imperial Rome. One does not have to do much research to find accounts of daily assaults on Christianity. During the week I wrote this passage, Muslims in Indonesia violently blocked Christians from attending church services; authorities in Laos arrested Thai students for participating in Christian services; the government of Iran destroyed historic Christian monuments; thugs assaulted priests in Hanoi; an Islamist terrorist group killed thirty-six Christians in an Easter Sunday attack.

These Christians continue to roar despite the threats. If they can do so, we have no excuse for staying silent here in North America. Typically, we fear little more than cold shoulders, angry e-mails, media slams, and the loss of tax exemptions, and yet that is often enough to keep many of us silent in the face of injustice and cultural degradation.

The Manhattan Declaration

Christians are standing up and speaking out. For two thousand years, we have been working tirelessly to protect the vulnerable and the marginalized, and for two millennia the enemies of God have been working to subvert us. For this reason, we must also labor to reinforce those traditions essential to the preservation of the Christian community and the spreading of God's Word throughout the world.

It was to this end that a group of prominent Christian leaders cooperated on what was called the "Manhattan Declaration," which they presented at a November 2009 press conference in Washington DC. Nearly five thousand words long, the declaration addressed the issues of life, marriage, and religious liberty. It strongly urged Christians to stand their ground and defend all three. "Courage is contagious," said Billy Graham. "When a brave man takes a stand, the spines of others are often stiffened."[3]

The declaration's preamble provided a perspective rarely found in contemporary Christian expression. It documented, much as we have done in previous pages, the extraordinary and indispensable contribution of Christians to the creation of a compassionate, just, and inclusive civil culture.

This includes everything from resisting Rome's infanticide practices in the days of the Roman Empire to preserving the literature and art of Western culture during the Middle Ages to helping establish the rule of law and balance of governmental powers in the modern era. The body of the Manhattan Declaration does not shy from tracing the flow of Christian activism to its source:

> We act together in obedience to the one true God, the triune God of holiness and love, who has laid total claim on

our lives and by that claim calls us with believers in all ages and all nations to seek and defend the good of all who bear his image. We set forth this declaration in light of the truth that is grounded in Holy Scripture, in natural human reason (which is itself, in our view, the gift of a beneficent God), and in the very nature of the human person.[4]

In other words, the power to act flows from God through the vertical plane of the cross and, at the nexus, moves along the horizontal plane to the larger community. Almost all efforts to do good that are not divinely inspired come to naught or erode in a second or third generation. For two thousand years, however, Christian churches have been and continue to be a generating force for an astonishing amount of good worldwide.

In the last decade alone, as the declaration made clear, Christians have done exceptional work, much of it unrecognized. In addition to the thousands of seemingly routine works of mercy done daily in any number of settings, Christians have battled human trafficking and sexual slavery, cared for those suffering with AIDS in Africa, provided clean water to developing nations, and found homes for thousands of children orphaned in the brutal chaos that still reigns in much of the world.

DEFENDING MARRIAGE

The more good the church does, however, the harder its foes work to undermine its values. Let me provide a real-life example of how this works. At the April 2009 Miss USA finals, an openly homosexual contest judge, the self-named Perez Hilton, asked Miss California, twenty-one-year-old Carrie Prejean, whether states should legalize same-sex marriage. The question was entirely inappropriate for a contest this superficial. Prejean answered politely and respectfully. She was by no means a scholar, but hers was a quiet roar of reason and reconciliation:

> Well I think it's great that Americans are able to choose one way or the other. We live in a land where you can choose same-sex marriage or opposite marriage. And, you know what, in my country, in my family, I think that, I believe that marriage should be between a man and a woman, no offense to anybody out there. But that's how I was raised and I believe that it should be between a man and a woman.[5]

Despite the fact that the majority of Californians had just given the same answer as Prejean on a state-wide referendum, Hilton reacted furiously. "She gave the worst answer in pageant history," he immediately blogged. "Miss California lost because she's a DUMB ☐☐☐☐, okay?" He reportedly gave Prejean a "zero" vote, which likely cost her the Miss USA crown. She was first runner-up. "If that girl would have won Miss USA I would have gone up onstage," Hilton continued, "and snatched that tiara off her head."

Hilton's rants got more and more vulgar because his colleagues in the world of entertainment did not see fit to tell him he was out of line. They may not have noticed. Vulgarity has become the norm in godless regions of the world such as Hollywood. They directed their anger instead at Prejean. "A lot of people are mad at you," her manager told her. He did not want her to attend the coronation ball. "I'm afraid of what might happen to you. You really shouldn't come."

Over the next several months, the Hollywood community

continued to attack and embarrass Prejean. The attacks would ultimately result in the loss of her Miss California crown. What made this doubly absurd was that just a few months earlier, then Senator Barack Obama was asked his opinion on gay marriage, and he answered almost exactly as Prejean had. "I do not support gay marriage," said Obama. "Marriage has religious and social connotations, and I consider marriage to be between a man and a woman."[6]

Despite his stand, Hollywood activists voted overwhelmingly for Obama, also a self-proclaimed Christian. They spared him their wrath, however, because they presumed he said what he did about marriage just to get elected. He hinted as much in his 2006 book, *The Audacity of Hope.* "I must admit that I may have been infected with society's prejudices and predilections and attributed them to God," he wrote explaining his gay marriage position, "in that Jesus' call to love one another might demand a different conclusion."[7]

A serious Christian, Prejean allowed herself no such wiggle room. She went on to write a book about her experience, married a pro football player, and had her first child. She will survive. The viciousness of the attack on her, however, sent a powerful message to others in the entertainment field. To stand up for your faith can cost you your career.

"I think my whole ordeal," wrote Prejean, "reveals just how the culture of political correctness uses shaming, blackmail, and other forms of emotional abuse to force people and organizations to either stick to our beliefs and suffer the consequences, or throw away our beliefs just to be left alone."[8]

Providentially perhaps, Obama's presence on the national ticket led to the victory of California's Proposition 8, the constitutional amendment that defined marriage as a union between a man and a woman. The majority of white citizens voted against it. The majority of black and Hispanic voters supported traditional marriage and voted for it. These voters turned out in record numbers to support Obama.

The Manhattan Declaration strongly defended traditional marriage, defined as "a conjugal union of man and woman, ordained by God from the creation, and historically understood by believers and non-believers alike, to be the most basic institution in society."

Just a decade ago, no one would have even thought to challenge marriage, so embedded was it in the culture as a good and a given. As late as November 2008, remember, President Obama was seemingly dead set against same-sex marriage. Progressives, however, saw an opening. By cloaking same-sex marriage as a civil right, in the spirit of the black civil rights movement, activists were able to persuade many well-meaning people that this subtle assault on marriage was a natural progression, even an advance in human tolerance and understanding.

Along with the carrot of self-esteem, activists lashed out with the stick of ritual defamation. As Carrie Prejean discovered, to oppose the progressive agenda on this issue was to be a hater, a homophobe, a bigot. No one wants to be called those names, especially when a corrupt media is amplifying the accusations. This relentless propaganda has eroded opposition to same-sex marriage even, incredibly, among people who once vocally opposed it. The Manhattan Declaration in no small part came to be to fortify Christian backbone on this and other critical issues.

Christians have a moral obligation to treat homosexuals with dignity and respect. "We have compassion for those so disposed," reads the Manhattan Declaration. "We respect them as human beings possessing profound, inherent, and equal dignity;

and we pay tribute to the men and women who strive, often with little assistance, to resist the temptation to yield to desires that they, no less than we, regard as wayward."

But let's face it, this issue is not really about homosexuality. It is about marriage. Radical leftists understand that marriage is the bedrock of Christian civilization. Mark 10:1–10 recounts the story of how Jesus was tested by some Pharisees who asked him whether it was lawful for a man to divorce his wife. They pointed out that Moses had allowed for just such a possibility. "It was because your hearts were hard that Moses wrote you this law," Jesus replied. He then cited Genesis in verses 6–9 and introduced an essential new understanding of God's plan for man:

> But at the beginning of creation God "made them male and female." "For this reason a man will leave his father and mother and be united to his wife, and the two will become one flesh." So they are no longer two, but one flesh. Therefore what God has joined together, let no one separate.

Any attempt to render this union trivial—either through easy divorce, cohabitation, polygamy, or same-sex "marriage"— not only affronts biblical Christianity, but it also unleashes havoc on the larger community. A home without both a mother and father is a sad thing. A neighborhood that lacks fathers is a threat to the health and safety of anyone who lives in it or near it. For the hard core, chaos is an opportunity for governments to seize power. They may mask their first steps as a top-down form of Christian charity, but at the end of the day serious Christians find themselves in jail—or worse. For this reason, the drafters of the Manhattan Declaration implore their fellow Christians to take this issue very seriously:

And so just as Christ was willing, out of love, to give Himself up for the church in a complete sacrifice, we are willing, lovingly, to make whatever sacrifices are required of us for the sake of the inestimable treasure that is marriage.[9]

Protecting Religious Liberty

Progressive activists are also using the same-sex marriage issue as a way to attack Christianity and to erode religious freedom. When a state passes a same-sex marriage bill, that bill potentially makes any church that refuses to marry people of the same sex an outlaw church. Certainly, these laws empower the opponents of religious liberty to classify the offending congregation as a hate group and the congregants themselves as bigots.

The influential "watchdog" group, the Southern Poverty Law Center, has already labeled pro-family churches in this manner. Dr. Patrick Wooden, pastor at the Upper Room Church of God in Christ in Raleigh, North Carolina, has let the SPLC hear his roar. He has been one of the leaders in the protest against the organization.

Wooden told the *Christian Post* that he had "deep respect for the time honored work of the SPLC." That much said, Wooden told the *Christian Post*, the SPLC deeply errs by comparing groups like the KKK and skinheads to "groups who simply believe in the biblical model of marriage."[10] He strongly rejected the notion that to disagree respectfully with the progressive agenda merits a "hate group" designation.

These conflicts are happening everywhere and in the most unlikely places. In April 2012, Hutchinson, Kansas, made the news when its Human Relations Commission offered new regulations, under which a church that made its facilities available to the general public would have to make them available to gay couples.

"[Churches] would not be able to discriminate against gay and lesbian or transgender individuals," Meryl Dye, a spokesperson for the commission, told FOX News. Knowing how to tweak a Christian conscience, Dye added, "That type of protection parallels to what you find in race discrimination."[11] In truth, the parallel is a false one, a subversive one. The Bible tells us that all men are brothers, that all people are one people. There are many admonitions against racial and ethnic exclusion. The Bible, however, does not equate ethnic discrimination with same-sex discrimination. No book written in any culture up to a few years ago made this case.

If enacted, the Hutchinson regulation would force churches to support gay nuptials. "It is a collision course between religious freedom and the LGBT agenda," said Matthew Staver, chairman of the conservative Liberty Counsel Action. "This proposed legislation will ultimately override the religious freedom that is protected under the First Amendment."[12]

As we have seen already, educators are also quick to advance the same-sex agenda in the classroom. As a result, every child in those classes who tries to defend the biblical truths he or she has learned at home or in church leaves the door open to mockery and academic failure. This is yet another way in which religious liberty is threatened.

The students attending the National High School Journalism Conference sponsored by the Journalism Education Association and the National Scholastic Press Association in April 2012 got an unwelcome jolt of this reverse bigotry. The speaker was a gay advocate named Dan Savage, the founder of a well-known anti-bullying project. He was alleged to be speaking about bullying. Instead, he became the bully he was claimed to be warning the kids about.

This unfortunate young man quickly turned his discussion to the Bible. With no apparent obligation to the truth, he claimed that people "often" cite the Bible as the reason they bully gay people. The solution he suggested for this imagined problem? "We can learn to ignore the □□□□ in the Bible about gay people."

Savage then profanely compared the Bible's admonitions about homosexuality to those about menstruation, masturbation, and eating shellfish. If that were not enough, he made the absurd and offensive claim that, as a symptom of its inherent evil, "The Bible is a radically pro-slavery document." What Savage did not say, and what few students would have known, is that the abolitionists pulled their inspiration from the Bible. As the Wilberforce example suggests, and as I will show in more detail later, Christians were the first and very nearly the only people to wage war on slavery.

To their credit, scores of students walked out as Savage was speaking. Their challenge, going forward, is to try to find the *Imago Dei*, the image of God, even in a person who taunts them as Savage did. The fierceness of his attack suggested a soul in turmoil, a soul crying out for help. Christians repudiate the attack and roar back as a lion would, but their goal is reconciliation, not revenge. They want to answer that cry. They want to make converts, not enemies.

Unfortunately, those students who remained seemed fully unaware of Savage's biblical ignorance. He even cited an avowed atheist, Sam Harris, as the source of his biblical information. These remaining students cheered and applauded Savage.

"What are the odds that the Bible got something as

complicated as human sexuality wrong?" Savage asked the students rhetorically. The answer? "100 percent." He then claimed that beatings of gay people were "justified by the Bible," and added, "People are dying because people can't clear this one last hurdle."[13] The hurdle in question is biblical truth. If the nation needed a dramatic visual manifestation of the progressive war on family, faith, and marriage, Savage supplied it in spades. He and his allies will not be content until they make that "hurdle" illegal.

Marriage represents just one front in a broad-based assault on religious liberty. On a number of other fronts, activists, continuously working through government, seek to weaken or eliminate those conscience clauses that give Christian institutions immunity from mandated unchristian activities.

For instance, after "non-discrimination" laws were enacted in Massachusetts, Catholic Charities reluctantly chose to end its adoption service rather than to place orphaned children in same-sex households in violation of their moral teaching. In New Jersey, a Methodist institution was threatened with the loss of its tax-exempt status when it refused to allow a facility it owned to be used for same-sex ceremonies. To appease the courts, the institution had to deny all couples access to the facility. In 2012, most dramatically, Obama's Secretary of Health and Human Services mandated that religious organizations, along with others, cover in their insurance plans the cost of providing services that they considered immoral such as contraception, sterilization, and abortion-inducing drugs.

At the same time the courts are imposing anti-Christian mandates on religious organizations, they are encouraging anti-Christian organizations to force the removal of Christian symbolism from the public square. The examples of this are too numerous and too depressing to list, but I would like to add one bit of irony here.

The courts often cite the Fourteenth Amendment to the Constitution as their authority to deny Christianity its place in public life. The drafters of that amendment intended to assure free slaves all the legal rights of other citizens, and so they wrote, "No State shall make or enforce any law which shall abridge the privileges or immunities of citizens of the United States."

Nearly sixty years after its passage, the Supreme Court got it into its head that the drafters of this amendment, in addition to protecting the rights of slaves, hoped to prevent states and municipalities from endorsing Christianity. The justices insisted that the First Amendment provision that *Congress* not make any law "respecting the establishment of religion or prohibiting the free exercise thereof" applied to local government as well.

Andrew Johnson was president at the time the Fourteenth Amendment was enacted into law. He supported its passage. This is the same Andrew Johnson who said, "Christ first, our country next"; the same Andrew Johnson who hoped "to take the flag of our country and nail it below the cross." Now, the courts are telling America that Johnson and his allies, the men who passed the Fourteenth Amendment through Congress, intended to see prayers banned in huddles at high school football games? I don't think so.

Unless kingdom Christians stand together and reject these affronts to religious liberty, anti-Christian activists and their unwitting allies in the media will persist. They will continue to demand one concession after another. The sanctions they impose will escalate from social ostracism to civil action to, quite possibly, trial and imprisonment. In Canada, Christian clergy have already been prosecuted for *reminding* their congregants of the biblical sanctions against homosexuality.

It does take some courage to make one's roar heard in the current atmosphere, but it takes less courage now than it will a few years down the road, when the cost of speaking out might be considerably higher.

CHAMPIONING LIFE

In 1973, in the famous case known as Roe v. Wade, Supreme Court activists wiped the laws of all fifty states off the books and declared abortion a constitutional "right." Not since the Dred Scott decision more than a century earlier—the one that declared slaves "property"—had the court done so much harm to so many people with one swipe of the pen.

In the years after Roe, the abortion industry and its allies in the feminist ranks and the media have fought a dirty war to keep abortion a "right" that cannot be challenged by voters. This is a war in which too many Christians have sought a draft deferment. We ought not have. No issue is more fundamental. The Manhattan Declaration speaks to this point:

> A truly prophetic Christian witness will insistently call on those who have been entrusted with temporal power to fulfill the first responsibility of government: to protect the weak and vulnerable against violent attack, and to do so with no favoritism, partiality, or discrimination.

Nowhere has this war been dirtier than the state of Kansas. This is ironic given that Kansas, the "Free State," has arguably the noblest founding of any state in the union. By way of background, Congress passed the Kansas-Nebraska Act in 1854, allowing the citizens of the two newly formed states to vote as to whether their state would be slave or free. This would not be an issue in Nebraska, whose courts ruled against slavery, but it would be in Kansas. Immediately after passage, pro-slavery settlers from neighboring Missouri began flooding in.

Not unlike the signers of the Manhattan Declaration, nineteen Protestant ministers in the Boston area distributed a circular urging their congregants to move to Kansas under the auspices of the New England Emigrant Aid Company, believing "that no Christian work demanded effort more than the work for peopling Kanzas (sic) with men and women who were resolved to make it free."[14]

Answering God's call, Christians from New England and elsewhere abandoned everything, pulled up stakes, and moved to Kansas to keep the state out of the hands of the slavers. As history recorded, the Christians prevailed in "Bleeding Kansas," but, as the name suggests, not without a great deal of hardship and bloodshed.

Eli Thayer, one of the leaders of the abolitionist forces, told Congress in 1858, "If we thank God for patriots, we should also thank Him for tyrants; for what great achievements have patriots ever made, without the stimulus of tyranny?"[15] That is similar to the situation the devoutly Christian Phill Kline faced when he first became a candidate for state attorney general in 2002.

Good looking and well spoken, Kline was a Republican in a red state, but many politicians of either party had long since sold their souls to maintain the power and perks of office. Being unapologetically pro-life, Kline had helped draft legislation several years earlier to discourage late-term abortions. The new law allowed them only to protect a woman's life or to prevent her from suffering "substantial and irreversible impairment of a major bodily function."

The new law should have put an end to the late-term business of Dr. George Tiller. At the time, his unscrupulous practice had made the unlikely Kansas the late-term abortion capital of the world. Women were coming from all over the world to Wichita because Tiller had learned to work the system to stay in business.

He donated enough money to the right people to make sure that the state's tough abortion laws went largely unenforced. When Kline threw his hat in the ring in 2002, Tiller tried to kick it out. He invested hundreds of thousands of campaign dollars to defeat Kline. Although Kline prevailed, the money turned a would-be landslide into a narrow victory. A less committed Christian would have read the leaves and avoided controversy, but Kline knew that Tiller had to be violating the law in the most lethal of ways.

The numbers coming out of Tiller's clinic had only been increasing since the tougher law had been put on the books. What Kline discovered when he finally secured Tiller's records was that the "doctor" was taking just about any reason a girl offered for wanting an abortion—for instance, "Horses are my life and having kids would mess that up for barrel racing"—and interpreting it as a "substantial and irreversible impairment of a major bodily function."

Given that babies fully ready to be born were routinely being murdered, Kline believed that both Tiller and Planned Parenthood both should have been held accountable to the law. When Kline began to take action, the other side came back hard. Kline began a descent into a hell orchestrated by Tiller's most powerful supporter, the Democratic governor of the state, Kathleen Sebelius.

With Tiller's money behind her, Sebelius persuaded a popular Republican politician to switch parties and run as a Democrat against Kline. A thoroughly corrupt media helped destroy Kline's reputation and push his opponent over the top. Indeed, for its slanted coverage of the campaign, the *Kansas City Star* won Planned Parenthood's top national honor for 2006.

Not content to drive Kline out of office and out of state, Sebelius and her cronies bankrupted Kline through an unending series of thoroughly bogus ethical charges that he was forced to fight on his own. In the process, they hoped to discourage any other state attorney general from doing what Kline had attempted to do. Kline remained undaunted. In a 2008 speech at the Eagle Forum in St. Louis, Kline summed up perfectly the message that lies embedded in the nexus of the cross:

> The foundation of law is truth, and the author of truth is almighty God. And without the recognition of the author, there is no law. Our calling is simple. It is to stand and proclaim truth and grace and have faith that God is always working his wonders. That is what gives us our boldness. That is what gives us our hope. That is what allows us to walk into the dark corners of the world and bring forth light.[16]

If Sebelius and her appointees in the state judiciary expected Kline to roll over like a lamb, they somehow confused themselves with the Good Shepherd. Kline roared back like a lion, unapologetic about his faith and his commitment to life. On the title page of his response to the state judiciary's disciplinary panel, he quoted Psalm 70, in which King David asks God, "May those who seek my life be put to shame and confusion; may all who desire my ruin be turned back in disgrace." The media were aghast.

Sebelius succeeded, at least temporarily, because too many of the good Christian politicians in Kansas watched her persecute the "extremist" Kline and said nothing for fear of being tarred by the media. As the Manhattan Declaration notes, elected officials of both major political parties have been "complicit in giving legal sanction to what Pope John Paul II described as 'the culture of death.'"

By remaining silent in Kansas, the Republican politicians allowed the Democrat Sebelius to become Obama's Secretary of Health and Human Services. In this position, she was able to manage the administration's war on religious freedom. Those Republicans have only themselves to blame.[17]

"As Christians, we take seriously the biblical admonition to respect and obey those in authority," reads the Manhattan Declaration. "Yet laws that are unjust—and especially laws that purport to compel citizens to do what is unjust—undermine the common good, rather than serve it." The declaration continues, "Through the centuries, Christianity has taught that civil disobedience is not only permitted, but sometimes required." The declaration closes with this powerful roar:

> Because we honor justice and the common good, we will not comply with any edict that purports to compel our institutions to participate in abortions, embryo-destructive research, assisted suicide and euthanasia, or any other anti-life act; nor will we bend to any rule purporting to force us to bless immoral sexual partnerships, treat them as marriages or the equivalent, or refrain from proclaiming the truth, as

we know it, about morality and immorality and marriage and the family. We will fully and ungrudgingly render to Caesar what is Caesar's. But under no circumstances will we render to Caesar what is God's.

11.

RECONCILING PLYMOUTH ROCK WITH JAMESTOWN

OUR FAITH IS TRANSPARENT, TRANSCENDENT, and transformational. Our faith teaches us to cross over obstacles, shout down walls, break through crowds, and walk on the impossible, even in the midst of storms. Our faith enables us to survive the fires of life, overcome the den of lions, silence the serpents, and outwit the fox. Our faith teaches us to see the invisible, embrace the impossible, and hope for the incredible.

Our faith prepares us for the flood and rewards us with a rainbow. Our faith provides the stones—some to speak to, others to throw, others to roll, and, above all, the living One to stand upon.

Our faith is the faith that first the Pilgrims and then the Puritans brought to the shores of New England. This may not be the only faith practiced in our nation, but it is the faith so secure in itself that it invites other faiths to compete in the free market of religious ideas. This extraordinary faith provided the moral and spiritual foundation for what we call the "American experience."

These deep Christian roots have helped make America a nation like no other. Some refer to our distinctive self-confidence as "American exceptionalism," the belief that God is uniquely guiding our destiny. George Washington certainly believed as much. In the aftermath of the successful American Revolution he said, "I am sure that never was a people, who had more reason to acknowledge a Divine interposition in their affairs, than those of the United States."[1]

Sitting with Marc Nuttle, former Reagan Administration official and liaison to the former Soviet Union, I heard the most concise definition of our exceptionalism that I have yet to hear. Marc looked at me and said, "Samuel, it's simple. We are the only nation that stands upon the belief that the hierarchical order of authority lies in the following: God over man and man over government."

Americans had been acknowledging God's hand for more than 150 years before the Revolution. In the early part of the seventeenth century, several efforts were made to establish colonies in the British-controlled areas of the New World. The colonies at Plymouth and at Massachusetts Bay were settled by a God-fearing people who braved the oceans not to gather riches but to practice their faith freely.

As these Bible-believing Christ followers were settling New England, a different class of people was settling the area around Jamestown, Virginia. These were entrepreneurs and men of commerce. Although at least nominally Christian, their colony had no larger purpose than to generate a return on their investors' dollars—or the seventeenth-century equivalent thereof. These settlers were seeking to enlarge the tent of economic opportunity and expand the coffers of England's powerhouse.

Without a doubt, the collective American experience stands

upon the foundational DNA of the initial major settlements of Jamestown and Plymouth Rock. In Virginia, the focus was on commerce, trade, markets, and profits. Up north, in New England, the Puritans focused on the free exercise of faith through the conduits of conversions, worship, community, and service.

In essence, our nation began with—and still reflects—the mitochondrial strains of faith and markets, prophets and profits, cathedrals and banks. At times it seems Plymouth Rock and Jamestown stand juxtaposed, seemingly at odds. A question arises now and has arisen throughout our history: Can these two threads coalesce around the nexus of the common good?

Yes, absolutely. Plymouth and Jamestown shared a common heritage. Although their focuses were obviously different, both were Christian colonies and both believed in free enterprise. As it happened, the intense nature of the New Englanders' faith, coupled with their prudence and fortitude, allowed New England to prosper while the Virginia colony struggled despite its much greater subsidy from the home country.

THE NEW ENGLAND EXPERIMENT

What the New England experiment established, for the first time anywhere, was that a free, God-fearing, sober, self-regulating people would almost inevitably create wealth. In time, Virginia would create great wealth as well, but theirs was created on the back of slavery, an unsustainable pathology and one from which we have never fully recovered.

The New England experience is worth exploring as it offers insights for a successful future. After a difficult sixty-six-day voyage on board the small, rickety *Mayflower,* a group of religious Separatists took shelter in what is now Provincetown Harbor. This was November in the year of our Lord, 1620. There, the Pilgrims, as they came to be known, authored and signed a social contract to govern themselves in this new land. This "Mayflower Compact" set the tone for the way Americans would see their relationship to God and how they would express it. It reads in part:

> Having undertaken for the Glory of God, and Advancement of the Christian Faith, and the Honour of our King and Country, a Voyage to plant the first Colony in the northern Parts of *Virginia*; Do by these Presents, solemnly and mutually, in the Presence of God and one another, covenant and combine ourselves together into a civil Body Politick, for our better Ordering and Preservation, and Furtherance of the Ends aforesaid.[2]

Observe that these original Pilgrims put "God" and "Faith" before "King and Country." Their agenda was not left or right, liberal or conservative. Theirs was the Agenda of the Lamb.

In those first few desperate years—nearly half the Pilgrims would die before Thanksgiving 1621—the Pilgrims struggled to find a way to honor the vertical and horizontal planes of the cross. Contrary to current beliefs, they immediately made peace with the local Indians and would not have survived without their help. In those first few years, internal strife caused most of their problems.

Colonel William Bradford, governor of the Plymouth Colony, described the nature of the conflict after the issue had been resolved. Bradford wrote the following in 1623; it took him and his colleagues fewer than three years to figure out how the real world actually worked and how to fix it. This passage is a little long and not the easiest to read, but it is one of the most important documents in the history of Christianity in America, so please give it your best:

> All this while no supply was heard of, neither knew they when they might expect any. So they began to think how they might raise as much corn as they could, and obtain a better crop than they had done, that they might not still thus languish in misery.
>
> At length, after much debate of things, the Governor (with the advice of the chiefest amongst them) gave way that they should set corn every man for his own particular, and in that regard trust to themselves; in all other things to go on in the general way as before. And so assigned to every family a parcel of land, according to the proportion of their number, for that end, only for present use (but made no division for inheritance) and ranged all boys and youth under some family. This had very good success, for it made all hands very industrious, so as much more corn was planted than otherwise would have been by any means the Governor or any other could use, and saved him a great deal of trouble, and gave far better content. The women now went willingly into the field, and took their little ones with them to set corn; which before would allege weakness and inability; whom to have compelled would have been thought great tyranny and oppression.
>
> The experience that was had in this common course and condition, tried sundry years and that amongst godly and sober men, may well evince the vanity of that conceit of Plato's and other ancients applauded by some of later times;

that the taking away of property and bringing in community into a commonwealth would make them happy and flourishing; as if they were wiser than God. For this community (so far as it was) was found to breed much confusion and discontent and retard much employment that would have been to their benefit and comfort. For the young men, that were most able and fit for labour and service, did repine that they should spend their time and strength to work for other men's wives and children without any recompense. The strong, or man of parts, had no more in division of victuals and clothes than he that was weak and not able to do a quarter the other could; this was thought injustice. The aged and graver men to be ranked and equalized in labours and victuals, clothes, etc., with the meaner and younger sort, thought it some indignity and disrespect unto them. And for men's wives to be commanded to do service for other men, as dressing their meat, washing their clothes, etc., they deemed it a kind of slavery, neither could many husbands well brook it.

Upon the point all being to have alike, and all to do alike, they thought themselves in the like condition, and one as good as another; and so, if it did not cut off those relations that God hath set amongst men, yet it did at least much diminish and take off the mutual respects that should be preserved amongst them. And would have been worse if they had been men of another condition. Let none object this is men's corruption, and nothing to the course itself. I answer, seeing all men have this corruption in them, God in His wisdom saw another course fitter for them.[3]

In short, what the Pilgrims did was to attempt an experiment in socialism—as Karl Marx might have phrased it, "From each according to his ability, to each according to his needs." It did not work. It never does. The effort failed to produce adequate food or other provisions. What it did produce was friction and jealousy. Bradford and his colleagues came to see the whole experiment as unnatural, even blasphemous. They learned that they were not "wiser than God." They learned, too, that "the taking away of property and bringing in community into a commonwealth" did not make them "happy and flourishing." Just the opposite, in fact, it made them unhappy and impoverished.

This is a difficult lesson to understand for those who preach "economic justice" and believe that government meets all the needs of its citizens. As Bradford learned, that does not necessarily work, even when tried by "godly and sober men." When tried by people hostile or indifferent to God, the results can be disastrous. That is why so much in America depends on people who extend the horizontal plane of the cross through their own enterprises. Yes, government has a role, but we cannot cede our own responsibility to its agents, who may or may not have the best interests of the suffering at heart.

CITY ON A HILL

If not a socialist paradise, what then could a godly America look like? Writing seven years after Bradford's essay on socialism, Puritan John Winthrop made a sophisticated attempt to answer this question. He served up his thoughts in the form of a sermon titled "A Model of Christian Charity," delivered while still on board the ship *Arabella*. He and his fellow Puritans were about to settle the Massachusetts Bay Colony. Although he did not belong to Bradford's denomination, Winthrop came to many of the same conclusions.

In his very first paragraph, Winthrop established that what we think of as economic equality is not exactly part of God's plan for man. "GOD ALMIGHTY in His most holy and wise providence," wrote Winthrop, "hath so disposed of the condition of mankind, as in all times some must be rich, some poor, some high and eminent in power and dignity; others mean and in submission."

That much said, Christians have a moral obligation to share what they do have. Here, Winthrop quoted Paul's first letter to the Corinthians: "Ye are the body of Christ and members of their part" (12:27). Winthrop explained this to mean that all parts of the body "being thus united are made so contiguous in a special relation as they must needs partake of each other's strength and infirmity; joy and sorrow, weal and woe."

Winthrop cited several biblical verses to reinforce his point:

1 John 3:16: "We ought to lay down our lives for the brethren."

Galatians 6:2: "Bear ye one another's burden's and so fulfill the law of Christ."

1 Corinthians 12:26: "If one member suffers, all suffer with it; if one be in honor, all rejoice with it."

Winthrop wrote eloquently and in much the same language used by those who translated the King James Bible. That being so, I see no need to paraphrase the vision that Winthrop had for this new colony. His own words more than suffice:

We must entertain each other in brotherly affection. We must be willing to abridge ourselves of our superfluities, for the supply of others' necessities. We must uphold a familiar commerce together in all meekness, gentleness, patience and liberality. We must delight in each other; make others' conditions our own; rejoice together, mourn together, labor and suffer together, always having before our eyes our commission and community in the work, as members of the same body.

It is at this point in his sermon that Winthrop moved to a fuller understanding of American exceptionialism. Not only did this new colony have a distinctive contract with God, but it also had a responsibility to make that contract a model for all to emulate. "For we must consider that we shall be as a city upon a hill," wrote Winthrop for the ages. "The eyes of all people are upon us."[4] Winthrop took this reference from the parable of salt and light in the Sermon on the Mount, "You are the light of the world. A city that is set on a hill cannot be hidden" (Matthew 5:14 NKJV).

This theme was preserved for the future by Francis Scott Key, who wrote what would become the national anthem as a poem in 1814. Although largely nationalist in tone, the "Star Spangled Banner" nevertheless makes a direct appeal for divine intervention. The final verse contains these lyrics:

> Blest with victory and peace, may the heav'n rescued land
> Praise the Power that hath made and preserved us a nation.
> Then conquer we must, when our cause it is just,
> And this be our motto: "In God is our trust."

This poem presumes little about America's relationship with God. Yes, we may be a "heav'n rescued land," one "made and preserved" by God, but we can expect to conquer only when our cause is "just." America's later anthems were even more specific in reinforcing the notion that God's good will had to be asked for and earned.

Consider the song "America," whose lines, "Our fathers' God to Thee, / Author of Liberty" make clear just who the life force is behind America's very existence. Written in 1831 by Samuel Francis Smith, the song concludes with a direct appeal for God's continuing good grace: "Long may our land be bright/ with freedom's holy light;/ protect us by thy might, great God, our King."

"America the Beautiful," whose lyrics were written in 1895 by Samuel Ward, continues the theme. In the first verse, Ward asked that God "shed his grace" on the nation. In the second verse, he asked, "God mend thine every flaw/ Confirm thy soul in self-control/ Thy liberty in law!" Here, Ward acknowledged human failings, even in an experiment as blessed as America's. In the penultimate verse, he asked for a particular blessing from God so that "selfish gain no longer stain/ The banner of the free!"

Perhaps the most popular of our anthems, "God Bless America," was written in 1918 as a call to arms during World War I. It was not released, however, until 1938 when composer Irving Berlin, who was Jewish, modified the song to serve as something of a protest to the Nazi ascendancy. This song would be forever identified with its original singer, Kate Smith, who was Southern, Catholic, and iconically large. The first verse, rarely sung, describes the song as a "solemn prayer." The second verse, the one we all know, asks specifically for divine guidance.[5]

"THIS LAND IS YOUR LAND"

Only one popular American anthem disassociates itself from God, and that is Woody Guthrie's 1956 classic, "This Land Is

Your Land." Although Guthrie tells us, "This land was made for you and me," he gives no hint of who might have made it. It should not be a surprise that Guthrie was an open sympathizer, if not a member, of the Communist Party throughout his adult life.

Guthrie's anthem owes less to his American precedents than it does to "La Marseillaise," the French national anthem written in 1792, adopted by the new Republican government in 1795, and originally titled, "War Song for the Army of the Rhine." In this bloody, vengeful song, there is only one reference to God, and that—"Grand Dieu!"—is more of a profanity than a prayer. The final verse appeals not to God, the "author of liberty" as he is described in "America," but to "Liberty" incarnate:

> *Join the struggle with your defenders*
> *Under our flags, let victory*
> *Hurry to your manly tone*
> *So that in death your enemies*
> *See your triumph and our glory![6]*

The French Revolution that inspired this song was a godless one, and the anthem reflects it. Its "Declaration of the Rights of Man and of the Citizen," written the same year our Constitution went into practice—1789—gives no due to the "Creator" as ours does. It does acknowledge a "Supreme Being," in whose presence the declaration had been drafted, but there is no implied relationship between that entity and the citizens of the state. "The principle of all sovereignty resides essentially in the nation," the French declaration insists. "No body nor individual may exercise any authority which does not proceed directly from the nation."

By contrast, the rights of American citizens are bestowed

"by their Creator," and they are thus "unalienable." The state cannot take them away. Although the US Constitution is more legalistic than the Declaration, its preamble notes that one of its purposes is "to secure the Blessings of Liberty." This reinforces the notion in the Declaration that our rights are a blessing bestowed by God.

Then, too, the very first dictate of the Constitution's very first amendment reads as follows, "Congress shall make no law respecting an establishment of religion, or prohibiting the free exercise thereof."[7] The founders understood how utterly essential the free practice of our Christian faith was to the success of our national enterprise.

Manifest Destiny

The one catchphrase that has come to represent American exceptionalism, especially in its expansionist phase, is "manifest destiny." The phrase was first coined in 1845 by an Irish American editorialist to justify the annexation of Texas and the Oregon Country. Our destiny, as John O'Sullivan and others saw it, was to stretch from "sea to shining sea," an idea preserved in "America the Beautiful."

Although Catholic by background, O'Sullivan was likely not a practicing one. The essay in which the phrase first appears, "Annexation," makes no reference to God or Christ. O'Sullivan asked only why citizens remained passive as other nations attempted to check "the fulfillment of our manifest destiny to overspread the continent allotted by Providence for the free development of our yearly multiplying millions."[8]

There are those who believe that America had already lost

its way by 1845, that its urge to conquer and expand had cost the nation its unique bond with God. The truth was that the nation had been at war with itself from the very beginning.

In 1628, William Bradford had to deal with a contingent of non-Pilgrims in his midst that had no use at all for a divine compact. They called their enclave "Merrymount" and were not shy about flaunting their paganism. "They also set up a maypole, drinking and dancing about it many days together, inviting the Indian women for their consorts, dancing and frisking together like so many fairies, or furies, rather; and worse practices," wrote an indignant Bradford. "As if they had anew revived and celebrated the feasts of the Roman goddess Flora, or the beastly practices of the mad Bacchanalians."[9] Rooted as it was in the demonic, Merrymount did not last long enough to matter.

The real strain on the divine compact had more of a foothold in reason. It derived from man's eternal desire to have more—more wealth, more power, more land. This desire ran up against the Agenda of the Lamb in the early 1830s when President Andrew Jackson authorized the Indian Removal Act that would lead to the infamous "Trail of Tears." To his surprise, Christian activists resisted, and the fervor of their protest alarmed him. Foremost among them was missionary leader and Christian editorialist Jeremiah Evarts. As was true for many activists of this era, Evarts had been energized by the Second Great Awakening.

Like Winthrop, Evarts believed that the United States had the moral obligation to be a "beacon of goodness" to the world, one that shone the light of justice and morality to every corner thereof. He feared God's punishment were we to ignore our calling. "May a gracious Providence avert from this country the awful calamity of exposing ourselves to the wrath of heaven," he wrote, "as a consequence of disregarding the cries of the poor and defenseless, and perverting to purposes of cruelty and oppression, that power which was given us to promote the happiness of our fellow-men."[10]

During the early years of the Republic, an even more intense battle was being waged between the pro-slavery forces and the Christians who opposed them. Although slavery has existed almost everywhere since the fall, abolitionism is a purely Christian invention. Thomas Jefferson, although not a particularly religious person, worried, as Evarts did, that America had violated its divine contract in its tolerance of slavery. As a slave owner, Jefferson had good reason to feel anxious. He wrote in his book, *Notes on the State of Virginia*:

> God who gave us life gave us liberty. And can the liberties of a nation be thought secure when we have removed their only firm basis, a conviction in the minds of the people that these liberties are of the Gift of God? That they are not to be violated but with His wrath? Indeed, I tremble for my country when I reflect that God is just; that His justice cannot sleep forever.[11]

The fight to free the slaves engaged Christian women as much as it did men and introduced them to the political battlefield, a place that they had not ventured previously in anyone's history. The most influential woman in the movement, perhaps the most influential person regardless of sex, was Harriet Beecher Stowe. Her best-selling 1852 novel, *Uncle Tom's Cabin*, alerted ordinary Americans to the human horror of slavery. Upon meeting Stowe, Abraham Lincoln was alleged to have said, "So this is the little lady who started this great war." About the book Stowe remarked, "I did not write it. God wrote it. I merely did his dictation."[12]

In the years following the Civil War, political factions struggled over the meaning of American exceptionalism. Some saw it in the same deeply Christian spirit as Winthrop and Bradford had. Others like O'Sullivan saw the concept in only vaguely Christian terms and added a more militant, even imperialistic twist. No one gave voice to this concept more thoughtfully than President Ronald Reagan. Consider the following from Reagan's announcement that he was running for president in November 1979:

> A troubled and afflicted mankind looks to us, pleading for us to keep our rendezvous with destiny; that we will uphold the principles of self-reliance, self-discipline, morality, and, above all, responsible liberty for every individual that we will become that shining city on a hill.[13]

Although not an explicitly Christian speech—Reagan cited Winthrop, not Jesus—the biblically literate knew Reagan's source and his inspiration. Like many of his forebearers, God's grace was not something Reagan took for granted. Reagan quoted the critical section in Winthrop's "city upon a hill" sermon where he said, "If we shall deal falsely with our God in this work we have undertaken, and so cause Him to withdraw His present help from us, we shall be made a story and a by-word through the world."[14] With God's blessing, both Winthrop and Reagan understood, comes responsibility.

Where America differs from the rest of the Western world is that the debate continues here and does so in a spirited way. The very diversity of Christian churches in the United States has helped us avoid the cold institutionalism of European state churches. Our churches still live; theirs do not. Indeed, it was not until 1954 that the phrase "under God" was added to the Pledge of Allegiance.

PUTTING EXCEPTIONALISM TO WORK

Imagine for a moment a self-ignited, collective community reinvestment act. Imagine that those who drafted the act did so not as a public relations strategy but rather to promote justice and charity. Now imagine this act as part of a corporate activities portfolio in which good works stand front and center as the primary metrics of efficacy and success. For we have always had, and always will have, both faith and free markets, Plymouth Rock and Jamestown. Can we see a movement that permits Jamestown to partner with Plymouth Rock? Yes. Can we do justice without dependence on big government? Yes we can! In truth, it is the only way we can.

George W. Bush attempted to lead such a reformation by framing the apparatus for what he called "compassionate conservatism." Yet, as it happened, his well-intended efforts almost deviated into enlarging the efforts of government. A secular government has no gift for reconciling Plymouth Rock with Jamestown. That effort has to spring from the people and their churches.

Bush also gave birth to a faith-based office stemming out of the executive branch. He introduced the idea of White House–directed faith initiatives. Although the larger idea seemed admirable, and many of the efforts such as the war on AIDS and malaria in Africa should be celebrated, the execution of the idea showed the temptations that arise when the faithful solicit funds on Capitol Hill.

UNCLE SAM'S TABERNACLE

Ideally, government partners with a church, synagogue, or mosque for community empowerment and renewal, not to endorse a belief, approve a sermon, or pick out songs from the hymnal. Ideally, too, the wall between church and state works both ways. It protects the government from establishing one religious belief system and usurping all other convictions, while shielding the church from the overreach of the state. This, of course, is the way it is supposed to work.

Unfortunately, money changes everything. More than ever, churches want to visit with Uncle Sam—not to ask the great Uncle to repent for millions of slaughtered babies, nor to demand that he cease inundating our public schools with anti-Christian, culturally deadening curricula. All too often, unfortunately, pastors and faith leaders climb the marble staircases of two-hundred-year-old secular temples to ask for one thing: a handout.

A few questions arise. One is whether churches that collaborate with the state should have to submit to federal regulations that require them to hire individuals whose very lifestyles run counter to church teachings. Uncle Sam in his most recent reincarnation certainly thinks so. In an unprecedented move, the Obama administration chose to sue a Lutheran school for dismissing a "commissioned minister" for breaking a particular church doctrine. The EEOC (Equal Employment Opportunity Commission) argued that since "ministry work" took up only forty-five minutes of the woman's workday, she was entitled to lost wages, damages, and attorneys' fees.

Fortunately, the Supreme Court thought otherwise. By a unanimous 9–0 vote, the Court ruled that "there is a ministerial exception grounded in the Religion Clauses of the First

Amendment" and that churches are free to hire ministers without government interference.[15] The troubling thing is that an elected administration felt free to pursue this course of action and suffered no consequence for doing so.

Even if the churches could trust the government, the question arises as to whether they should be asking Uncle Sam for funding in the first place. There are obvious problems involved. If Uncle Sam decides to partner with Reverend Smith, Rabbi Goldstein, or Imam Ali, that collaboration will require either conformity to religious tenets on the state's part or subjugation to federal law on the part of the religious organization. Something has to give, and it is unlikely to be the government. This awkward and uncomfortable collaboration will almost inevitably result in a faith that sacrifices doctrinal purity for the sake of financial gain.

Accordingly, we should ask, whatever happened to the biblical injunction to "render unto Caesar what belongs to Caesar and to God what belongs to God?" Why are faith-based groups begging Uncle Sam for crumbs when, by our very nature, we should be looking only to the Lord for sustenance? As we know from the Gospels, five loaves and two fishes resulted in twelve baskets of crumbs, and this was after five thousand people had been fed. That was a miracle, of course, and something we cannot expect on a routine basis. What this episode teaches us, though, is that faith in Jesus Christ will always be rewarded in one way or another.

Let me be clear. I have no problem if Uncle Sam comes to the church and recognizes that faith-based groups execute ministries to the poor and hurting in a more constructive and holistic manner than government ever can. After all, this is our mission. From Isaiah 61 to Luke 4 and Matthew 25, all major Christian narratives stand spiritually and morally committed to the restoration of lives and the renewing of dreams.

Matthew 25 is particularly instructive on this front. Here, Jesus describes the eternal reward for those who tended to Jesus when he was in need:

> I was hungry and you gave me something to eat, I was thirsty and you gave me something to drink, I was a stranger and you invited me in, I needed clothes and you clothed me, I was sick and you looked after me, I was in prison and you came to visit me. (Matthew 25: 35–36)

In referring to himself in this context, Jesus really meant all of humankind—"whatever you did for one of the least of these brothers and sisters of mine, you did for me." This is what Christians do. Thus, I find it entirely contrary to the spirit of the Bible for a faith-based group to approach government and beg for funding to accomplish a divine mandate of charity and compassion.

Needless to say, Jesus never told his followers that it was Caesar's job to feed the hungry and tend to the sick. Nor did he tell his followers it was their job to lobby Caesar to raise taxes so that the Roman Empire could do this more lavishly. He never talked about a "Buffet Rule" or its first-century equivalent in which we coerce others to give what we cannot or will not. No, if we accept subsidies from Caesar, we agree to play by Caesar's rules, and his rules are not anything like our rules.

As rule maker, moreover, the government will always be tempted to insist on changes. If the churches enter a contract with the government, they are all but obliged to comply. Here in America we do not yet know whether churches and other faith organizations will ignore their religious beliefs and abandon claims to religious freedom in order to receive government money. What we do know from history is that governments will favor those religions that shape their beliefs along state-approved lines. To see how this works, study the fate of the German Christian Church in the 1930s and 1940s or the state-approved "patriotic" churches in contemporary China.

Serving raises yet another question. Faith-based organizations that receive government funds are obliged to serve the entire community, regardless of sex, race, or sexual orientation. That is not a problem. Christ calls upon us to serve all those in need unconditionally. Service speaks to mission—a mission that both government and church agree should be rendered to all. But those who serve should reflect the spirit of the servant church. A state that forbids prayer in school does not like it any better in a homeless shelter. Our need to promote our mission offends the state.

Despite the uneasy relationship between church and state, collaboration sometimes makes sense. After Hurricane Katrina in 2005, for instance, when the government seemed paralyzed by ineptitude, the faith community mobilized instantly. Organizations like the Convoy of Hope were tending to the sufferers while FEMA (Federal Emergency Management Agency) was still trying to locate New Orleans on the map. The state should partner with the institutions of faith that have historically serviced the needy with a greater reliability and effectiveness than any government agency, but the state should ask no more of that organization than its help. Once the state accepts that help, it should cease to make demands. The state should remember who is helping whom.

If a faith-based organization must subscribe to a set of government-sponsored values as a prerequisite for subsidies, perhaps welfare beneficiaries and other recipients of government aid should do the same. This is absurd, of course, but no more absurd than asking a church to forego its values for a subsidy. Collaboration should not require the sacrifice of conviction. The state should concern itself only with incorporating complementary skills that converge around the epicenter of effectiveness. If Uncle Sam wants our help, then we will assist. However, he should not require us to change our beliefs or surrender our theological doctrine at the altar of financial expediency. If he does, we should refuse to participate.

Are We Still Exceptional?

Two objects cannot occupy the same space. This simple law of physics should instruct us and guide us as we deliberate in the midst of so much change. We are either an exceptional country or we are not.

Yet the nation is obviously in the throes of change. Some of those changes represent forward motion. We overcame slavery and segregation. We overcame the Great Depression and defended democracy in World Wars I and II. We successfully confronted and defeated global Communism, and we currently stand poised to push back on religious totalitarianism.

Nevertheless, our current sociopolitical reality prompts us to ask some very important questions. What makes us different as a nation? Do we truly stand as the bastion of democracy for all to follow? Are we still "the City on a Hill?" Does the notion of American exceptionalism make sense in the twenty-first century?

The debate as to whether or not we are still exceptional rages even today and has been joined by a third party, the noisy one that does not think America ever was exceptional in the first place. That faction faults us for following Christ, not Marx. Nothing we can do will satisfy them.

I believe that we retain the potential to stay atop the hill. The incorporation of a moral framework as it pertains to the economic markets of our nation, one which empowers the entrepreneur, facilitates free markets, addresses poverty and inequality, serves the community, and seeks to enrich all Americans will serve as a firewall against an ever-encroaching government. It will also temper greed, undermine ubermaterialism, and steer us away from apathy.

There are no guarantees. Our relationship with God demands constant vigilance. From the very beginning we have been worrying about our potential to fall away. George Washington said the following of his fellow citizens after acknowledging the "Divine interposition" in American affairs: "I should be pained to believe that they have forgotten that agency, which was so often manifested during our Revolution, or that they failed to consider the omnipotence of that God who is alone able to protect them."[16]

If we deviate from the premise that in America God is over man and man is over government, we will not last long as a nation. The rejection of this foundational framework will surely result in chaos, angst, and the potential termination of our noble experiment. This does not have to happen.

12.

RECONCILING *IMAGO DEI* WITH *HABITUS CHRISTUS*

DO NOT CRUCIFY WHAT GOD RESURRECTS AND do not resurrect what God crucifies. Our movement, the Lamb's Agenda, must stand committed to reconciling the vertical *Imago Dei*, the image of God in every human being, with the horizontal *habitus Christus*, the habits and actions of Christ. This requires a new narrative, an alternative discourse where we stand for truth without sacrificing civility.

The image of God lives in all human beings: black and white, rich and poor, straight and gay, conservative and liberal, citizen and undocumented. Our challenge is to see the image of God in every human being including those we disagree with. Our challenge is to see the image of God even in those who persecute and slander us. Our challenge is to see the image of God in those who oppose us. Our challenge is to see the image of God in the suffering, the marginalized, the oppressed, and the hurting. Our challenge is to see the image of God in friend and foe, acquaintance and stranger, strong and weak, oppressor and liberator.

"Father, forgive them," said Jesus of his tormentors even as he hung in agony on the cross, "for they do not know what they are doing" (Luke 23:34). As was true for Jesus, "Our struggle is not against flesh and blood, but against the rulers, against the authorities, against the powers of this dark world and against the spiritual forces of evil in the heavenly realms" (Ephesians 6:12).

As has been true for ages, segments of our community, sometimes very powerful segments, torment those who do not espouse a biblical worldview. The Lamb's Agenda requires—no, it demands—that we view the other through the lenses of grace and compassion, the *Imago Dei*.

Then the question must be asked, who are the true enemies of the Lamb's Agenda? Moral relativism, spiritual apathy, lukewarm faith, cultural decadence, needless poverty, injustice, racism, discrimination, intolerance, complacency, bitterness, fear, hatred, animosity, lies, strife, discord, sin, and terror—these are the true enemies of our faith. As we fight them, we cannot allow ourselves to become them.

RHETORICAL PORNOGRAPHY

For that matter, we must push back against what might be called "rhetorical pornography," an indulgence in a language that is meant to inflict emotional pain.

We've all heard this saying since we were school kids knocking around in the playground: "Sticks and stones will break my bones, but words will never hurt me." The intent behind this saying is a good one to be sure. We say it to steel young minds and hearts against the inevitable bruises of childhood and adolescence. Even the coolest kids get called names. The vulnerable, the uncool among them, suffer incalculable verbal abuse.

As hard as we might try, did any of us ever believe name-calling did not hurt? Even today—now that we are older, hopefully wiser, having experienced the heartaches of everyday life more fully than we may have as kids—is "words will never hurt me" a maxim we can stand behind? The Lamb's Agenda says no. Words do hurt, and we should not be the ones inflicting the pain.

Just about every day, a quick scan of the news headlines, or a couple of keystrokes for a Google search, serve up stories proving this old adage false. The evidence can come from picket signs, from talk-show sound bites, from not so funny jokes, from something as short and simple as a 140-character tweet.

Protestors in Arizona clash over immigration policy. Public arguments flare up over homosexuality in California. Debates rage about Obamacare in the nation's capital. The list goes on. Some of the name-callers are well known and have even built reputations on their willingness to call people out. Some well-known people can be very nearly as abusive but convince themselves they are not. You can name a dozen examples of each.

Most of those doing the name-calling, however, are unknown beyond their own limited circles. In the age of social media—an age in which everyone has instant access to a public, and many of the most vocal hide behind a phony name—the language has grown more violent, more vulgar, more hard-core rhetorically pornographic. Well known or not, the actions of the name-callers prove a singular truth: names do hurt—and not just those on the receiving end of them.

Let me cite one name out of the news as an example, that of Bernie Madoff, the financier who swindled thousands of people, many of them friends, out of billions of dollars. One cannot begin to justify what he did. And although he wrecked a lot of dreams, he dealt almost exclusively with people of means. He killed no one, molested no one, abused no one. Yet when I Googled "Bernie Madoff" and "hate," I got 670,000 hits.

His daughter-in-law wrote, "I hate Bernie Madoff." *Business Week* personal finance editor Lauren Young wrote "Why I Hate Bernie Madoff." A YouTube video was titled "Everybody hates Bernie Madoff." Read deeper into the diatribes and you find people expanding their hatred from Madoff to Wall Street, to all rich people, to Jews, to people who hate people who hate Jews, to people who hate people who hate Wall Street. "Madoff is like Emmanuel Goldstein in the novel *1984*," wrote Kyle Smith in *Forbes*—"the guy all are instructed to hate without being told exactly why."[1]

Although a strong word in itself, *hate* is among the least of the vitriol thrown Madoff's way. The blog posts about him are laced with casual profanity, gratuitous insults, and anti-Semitic rants by people who never knew Madoff and never invested with him.

To paraphrase another old aphorism: what we say about others reveals more about ourselves than the people we're talking about. This is especially true for Christians, who encounter any number of verses in the Bible that ask for restraint in speech. "The wise in heart are called discerning," says Proverbs 16:21, "and gracious words promote instruction."

Jesus, as we know, tended to be a bit more direct. As noted in Matthew 12:36–37, Jesus said, "But I tell you that everyone will have to give account on the day of judgment for every empty word they have spoken. For by your words you will be acquitted, and by your words you will be condemned."

Today, given the electro-charged public square in which we

speak, our words can cause enormous damage to any number of people within seconds of leaving our mouths. Once gone, there is no pulling them back, no erasing them. They may live in the cybersphere forever. As Christians, we should not add useless wind to this electronic maelstrom. We should measure our language, especially in assessing our critics. Derogatory terms for other human beings, regardless of how widely their views differ from ours—or, more importantly, from the truths of Scripture—should not pass through our lips.

As suggested earlier, the catch phrase "rhetorical pornography" works all too well. For this kind of language debases the speaker and the one spoken to, the former even more than the latter. To get into the terms too specifically here would be to attach to them a dignity they don't deserve. But, like pornography itself, we know rhetorical pornography when we are exposed to it.

We have all heard the hateful epithets and cutting adjectives directed at gays and lesbians that go far beyond reasoned articulation of our biblical views about God's design for human sexuality. Even if their supporters cruelly attack our views, it does not justify our retaliation in kind.

I have heard any number of dismissive descriptions for those who do not share our faith or for those who do not have any faith at all. When we use these, we drive the insulted even further from the heart of Christ, the exact opposite of our calling as his modern-day disciples. Let me repeat: we are here to make converts, not enemies. A well-targeted zinger may satisfy our need for revenge, but for a Christian there can be no target other than the soul. If a comment is well targeted, the recipient will not feel insulted, but consoled.

Perhaps most distressing, and most common, are ethnic slurs against the most vulnerable among us, particularly those noncitizens whose every day in our country can be an anxious struggle. We can harbor a range of opinions on immigration policy, but as Christians we know of only one way to treat immigrants themselves—those who have families like our own and are working as hard to feed them as we are—and that is the way Jesus would.

As we know, Jesus did not discriminate. In John 4, he stopped by Jacob's well, which was manned by Samaritans, historic enemies of his people. When a Samaritan woman came to draw water, Jesus shocked her by asking, "Will you give me a drink?" Aware of the division between them, she answered, "You are a Jew and I am a Samaritan woman. How can you ask me for a drink?" Jesus explained to her that there were no longer artificial ethnic divisions, "but whoever drinks the water I give them will never thirst. Indeed, the water I give them will become in them a spring of water welling up to eternal life." His fountain is open to all.

Any words that are used to render people faceless, to deny them their innate humanity, to undo their inherent dignity are words that should not flow from a Christian mouth. The Jesus we follow did not die only for those of us who look like him or even those who believe in him. His Father created each one of us in his own image, *imago Dei,* and he embraces all of us whether we want to be embraced or not.

This means that as Christ breathed his last on the cross, he had as much love in his heart for the undocumented immigrant as he had for the border patrol officer, as much for the homosexual activist as for the stalwart defender of traditional marriage, as much for the atheist as for the Bible-believing pastor. This is not an easy concept to accept. It wars with our nature, but it is a battle we must fight and, ideally, win.

"For the mouth speaks what the heart is full of," said Jesus in

Matthew 12:34. What Jesus meant was that it is far more than a failure of tone when we marginalize or malign those with whom we disagree. The solution is not just "nicer" words but a transformed perspective—a more acute vision—one that sees all human beings, including opponents, through the eyes of our *proponent*, Jesus.

Accordingly, we must repudiate all vestiges of articulated terror. Let a generation arise who will dare to speak to both the heathen and the Pharisees. Let a generation arise committed to turning the table of the money-changer in the temple and to writing on the ground while saying, "He who is without sin, throw the first stone." The day of angry evangelicalism is officially over. The day of a loving, Bible-believing community espousing truth with love officially commences right now. For if we truly understand that every human being is made in God's image, then we can proceed to advance the Lamb's Agenda.

THE HABITS OF CHRIST: FORGIVENESS

Nations launch wars. Governments persecute the innocent. Institutions reinforce hatred. But as to the children of God, what we do is forgive. It is this very act of forgiveness that removes the grave clothes of bitterness and reveals a glimmer of hope, a rebirth of faith, a new beginning in Christ.

Habitus Christus, the habits and actions of Christ, are our ultimate guide. They require that forgiveness be our ultimate qualifier, the bar we must get over. Our movement will be known for many things, but none more distinctive than forgiveness.

The greatest, most provocative single action any human can take upon this planet is to forgive. Nelson Mandela invited his former captors to his presidential inauguration. Gandhi called for Hindus and Muslims to reconcile. Pope John Paul II met with his would-be assassin, Mehmet Ah Agca, and forgave him for the shooting while Agca, in turn, pressed the Pope's hand against his forehead, a symbol of respect for Muslims.

That these incidents stand out reminds us that in a world whose narrative is written in the blood of war, terrorism, strife, and hatred, genuine apostles of forgiveness are rare. They are not so rare, though, that they cannot serve as models of mature and balanced relationships at all levels—personal, corporate, geo-political, economic, and ecclesiastical. All participants in these relationships are obliged to forgive. All are obliged to exercise mercy in the presence of justice. All are obliged to transcend the hurt and the pain as Jesus did on the cross.

To be sure, even those who do not receive earthly justice can forgive and should forgive. The world advances, however, when forgiveness follows justice. Forgiveness without justice grants an evil, unjust clemency. From the Holocaust to Rwanda, from Darfur to Serbia, when jurisprudence speaks on behalf of the innocent while confronting evil, justice ensues, and justice is the great facilitator of forgiveness. Those who stand responsible for atrocities, murder, and mayhem must receive the legal and moral consequences of such actions. Soon thereafter, the victims are called to forgive while the rest of us are admonished not to forget. Atrocities prove we are fallen creatures, imperfect and prone to cruelty. Forgiveness proves we are still children of a righteous God.

The Prescription for Spiritual Myopia

At one time or another, spiritual myopia afflicts us all. We fail to see the moral landscape in its entirety, often because we choose not to. We can ease this affliction only through the corrective lenses of righteousness and justice, the *imago Dei* and *habitus Christus*. Today, the moral, political, and social haze that obscures the vision of all of us demands this one reliable prescription if we are to identify the ills afflicting humanity, let alone address them. The optics of holiness and humility always succeed in correcting spiritual myopia, cultural vertigo, willful blindness.

The good Dr. Luke, in Acts 17:28, attached with surgical precision a simple truth to the spiritual body of our journey: "For in him we live and move and have our being." This simple yet powerful truth guides us to an unshakable conviction. In him—not in religion built around him, not in wars fought in his name, not in exercises of grandeur, not in dogmatic systems, not in hierarchical bureaucracies, but in him—we live. In his humility, love, mercy, grace, and compassion, we live. We live when we embrace his nature, his mission, and his sacrifice. We live in his directives to love our neighbor, to love even our enemies, to turn the other cheek, all the while walking justly before our God.

We move in his character, his holiness, his righteous indignation against the pharisaic spirit. We move in his journey from Bethlehem to Golgotha and all points in between. We move in his encounters with the rich and the poor, with peasants and political leaders, with sinners and saints. We move in his passion for all God's children to be free. Every opportunity to forgive, assist, and heal presents an invitation to move in him.

Finally, in Christ we have our being. Descartes declared, "I think therefore I am." Pascal countered, "I believe therefore I am." My response in the midst of moral relativism, social, political, and economic uncertainty is simple: "Christ, therefore I am." The prescription is simple: live in his image, walk in his Spirit, exist in his grace.

13.

THE NEXUS OF
THE CROSS

THE NEXUS OF THE CROSS IS THE PLACE WHERE
conviction marries compassion, where the fish intersects with
the bread, where truth joins hands with mercy, where we reconcile the optics of redemption with the metrics of reconciliation.

The nexus is the place where a balanced soul finds its home,
where faith meets action, conviction greets compassion, and the
prophetic intersects with the practical. The nexus is the strongest
part of the cross, the intersection of righteousness and justice,
the platform where heaven touches earth, and the womb from
which the Lamb's Agenda flows.

THE PROPHETIC CENTER

The nexus of the cross is nothing other than the prophetic center. I am not speaking here of a muddy and ambiguous political
center where, on occasion, compromise quenches conviction,

but of a genuine prophetic center where obedience always meets sacrifice.

Once again, I am thoroughly convinced that the current religious debate in America is not a bilateral conflict between Christ's followers and their foes on the political left, as the media often suggest, nor even a struggle between church and state. No, America's debate on religion is trilateral. The twenty-first century finds three forces contesting in the public square: religious secularism, religious pluralism, and religious exceptionalism.

The secularists enter the fray with little support, less endurance, and the least possible hope of victory. This nation may not officially be a Christian nation, but it is a nation where the majority still self-identify as followers of Christ. Even though no one religion monopolizes the public square, one cannot deny that our nation embraces spirituality. The survey numbers cited earlier bear witness to this. Despite all the media attacks on Christianity, more than three-fourths of Americans still identify themselves as Christian.

Our founding fathers, whether Deists or Christians, inscribed a faith narrative that cannot be denied. From the beginning, as we have seen, faith, spirituality, and the actual practice of religion affect public discourse, elections, politics, and foreign affairs, not usually as the centerpiece of policy, but almost always as one of the elements that shapes the norms and mores by which policy is written. One cannot extract from our ethos the spiritual thread woven into the American genome.

While France and other European nations treat religion as an historical artifact and have stripped even the vestiges of spirituality from public life, and while Iran and a score of other countries actively persecute religious minorities, our nation thrives through religious pluralism and tolerance.

Consequently, our greatest export may not be technology, popular culture, or our brand of democracy but rather a commitment to religious pluralism, diversity, and tolerance—a commitment that stems directly from our Judeo-Christian value system. In other words, the nexus of the cross empowers us to propose—not impose—a simple proposition, namely, as John tells us in his memorable 3:16, "For God so loved the world that he gave his one and only Son, that whoever believes in him shall not perish but have eternal life."

THE HOME OF PURE CHRISTIANITY

The nexus is more about relationship than religion. Religion, as practiced, is purely man made. For that reason, religion can never be perfect. Our attempt to contextualize a religious system, a set of beliefs or programs to manage and understand God, continuously falls short. How could it not? Our powers of understanding are painfully limited. Even our best scientists cannot begin to decipher life on earth, let alone the beginning of the universe. We are nowhere near ready to understand God in all his fullness.

The New Testament defines pure religion by our treatment of those in need. Once again, this is what makes *pure* Christianity so attractive. The nexus of the cross is the domicile of pure Christianity. What Christ introduced was less of a religion than a relationship. To some, the ministry of Christ expresses God's desire to introduce humanity and the world to a revolutionary relationship simple in expression, awesome in power, and magnificent in grace.

Christ transformed the conversation from ritual, especially those rituals stripped of humanity, to relationship. In Luke, for instance, Jesus asked the Pharisees if it is lawful to heal on the Sabbath. But this simple act of humanity confounded their system of laws, so Jesus went ahead and healed a man of his abnormal swelling. He then shared with them the parable of the wedding feast, concluding:

> When you give a luncheon or dinner, do not invite your friends, your brothers or sisters, your relatives, or your rich neighbors; if you do, they may invite you back and so you will be repaid. But when you give a banquet, invite the poor, the crippled, the lame, the blind, and you will be blessed. Although they cannot repay you, you will be repaid at the resurrection of the righteous. (Luke 14:12–14)

These are the relationships on which Christianity is based: the unexpected ones, the uneasy ones, the unrewarding ones—unrewarding at least from any material perspective. This relationship-based faith flummoxed the Pharisees and continues to unsettle their twenty-first-century heirs. Yes, there is a place for ritual, but ritual without relationship is as spiritually hollow today as it was two thousand years ago.

All religions may reflect the same spiritual hunger apparent in every human being, but not all religions are equally valid. Good religions attempt to answer the questions of heaven and earth—"Does life exist beyond us?" Great religions ask, "Does something greater exist inside us?" Grace empowers them to pose tougher questions still, like "What do we need to do to be saved?" and "Who is the greatest amongst us?" These questions lead Christians to understand the one relationship that inspires all other relationships, and that inspiration stems from the nexus of the cross.

MORE POWERFUL THAN THE EXTREME

From the nexus of the cross, the followers of Christ learn to repudiate any extreme, left or right, that asks its adherents to ignore the virtues of love, compassion, and forgiveness. This is not a lesson learned easily. Christians, like members of all religions, have competing passions. Although they rarely ever admit it, many followers of Christ identify more strongly as Democrats or Republicans than they do as Christians. The more extreme the political identification—socialist, say, or libertarian—the more likely the person is to advance a political agenda before the Agenda of the Lamb.

At times in Christian history, the all-out politicization of the faith message has intensified hatreds, increased intolerance, and often ended in bloodshed. As a result, those who dislike religion get to blame religion for the world's mayhem. They should be blaming human nature.

When stirred by old grudges or keen on power plays, combatants will adopt whatever ideological cover best fits their needs—and religion is often handy. In some religions, wars are fought in better conscience than in our own because the faithful preach love, compassion, and forgiveness only among members of their own community. When God is forced out of the equation altogether as happened in revolutionary France, Nazi Germany, Maoist China, and the Soviet Union, then blood flows as it never has before.

Christians have no excuse for failing to promote the Lamb's Agenda. Our faith goes beyond the framework of self-preservation. If we truly grasp that faith, we extend love, compassion, and forgiveness toward all. In the end, if the efforts to establish these virtues fail to unite the world's major religions, then the leaders of these religions, ours included, have failed their followers. When, however, the oracles of love, compassion, and forgiveness outnumber the prophets and evangelists of hatred and intolerance, then religion may very well trump human nature and succeed in reconciling God's children to one another.

This is the only way genuine peace will sweep the planet. Our secular friends can sing "give peace a chance," chant "hare, hare Krishna," and display "Coexist" signs proudly on their bumper stickers, but sustainable reconciliation can only emerge from of the nexus of the cross.

The Antidote to Extremism

When we consider a region of the world where religious ideas have been hijacked by extremists, we immediately think of the Middle East. There, extremism and religious discord are used to reinforce political platforms. It is a shame. As the birthplace of the world's three most prominent faiths, the region should be a vibrant marketplace of faith possibilities as diverse and cooperative as those in, say, New York, but even more sacred. Instead, to a large degree, the area remains a battlefield. At times, the "faithful" here communicate not through ecumenical gatherings but through Qassam rockets and IEDs.

To the outsider, these may seem like religious conflicts, but they are not, not really. If the 9/11 terrorists wanted to attack Christians, they would not have chosen a stronghold of secular finance like the World Trade Center in New York. Correspondingly, when terrorists bomb a school bus in Israel or a pizza place, they are sending a political message, not a religious one. Many of the most notorious terrorists are not religious at all. Some are not even Muslims.

To understand the political, moral, and socioeconomic dynamics that drive the region, observers cannot ignore that religious rationales are masking political and military conflicts. They must understand that the true conflict pits poverty and authoritarianism on the one hand against freedom and peace on the other. Rather than face internal problems, despots fix their followers' gaze on external enemies. This practice has been going on since long before Machiavelli drew attention to it nearly five hundred years ago.

Meanwhile, in the birthplace of monotheism, where his name is invoked daily, God sometimes seems like a prisoner of war. Only a Lamb's Agenda, one that flows from the nexus of the cross, can bring freedom to a region tormented by radical politics in the guise of religious extremism.

STRONG ENOUGH TO BE TESTED

The nexus of the cross makes our Christian message unique. While most other faiths avoid inquiries, Christianity invites them. Faith that is questioned is faith perfected. Questioning the tenets of faith will either solidify belief or guide one to another faith more open to such inquiries.

Throughout the biblical narrative and even today, God and his children have continued to participate in a dialogue. The great query presented in the garden of Eden by God—Where are you?—continues to resonate for humanity today. Humankind responds as it has for thousands of years: "What do we need to do to be saved?"

God is not afraid of our inquiries. The question we must ask ourselves is whether we are we afraid of his. If questioning exposes truth, let us question. A faith that is threatened by doctrinal inquiries and evaluation of certain tenets is no faith at all. A faith that blindly demands belief subjugates the very inquisitive soul that God gave us. What is more, it disqualifies itself from being a faith and more accurately falls under the category of a cult. True faith welcomes questions; false faiths discourage and prohibit them.

Let us not forget that if all the questions are answered and all doubts quelled, then we have not asked enough questions. We have satisfied ourselves too easily. On this earth, we will never know God in all his glory—we cannot. Faith thus remains the assurance of things hoped for and the conviction of things unseen.

MOTHER TERESA'S *VIA DOLOROSA*

An excellent example of a nexus-driven ministry is that of Mother Teresa. She described herself as an Albanian by birth, an Indian by citizenship, and a Catholic nun by faith. "As to my calling," said Mother Teresa, explaining the nexus of the cross with perfect simplicity, "I belong to the world. As to my heart, I belong entirely to the Heart of Jesus."

Mother Teresa grew in strength even as she struggled with her standing at the nexus of faith. If Job could question the plan of Providence and if Jesus could cry out, "Father, Father, why hast thou forsaken me?" then Mother Teresa could, without tarnish or shame, be admired despite her doubts and fears.

In fact, such personal struggles may demonstrate proof of the miraculous in her life. Mother Teresa walked on her own *Via Dolorosa*, the "way of grief" that Jesus walked on his way to Calvary. Mother Teresa's personal writings reveal a woman who not only questioned God on occasion, but who also doubted herself at times.[1]

This petite, fragile woman demonstrates to all of us, even after death, that one can muster strength despite doubt and perhaps even because of it. She gave hope when at times she had no hope to give. She witnessed her faith even as she wrestled with unbelief. She spoke on behalf of peace when her soul was at war. She took care of the orphans when she felt orphaned by her own heavenly Father.

One of the qualifications for sainthood in the Catholic Church is the validation of miracles in the midst of one's ministry. What greater miracle can one demonstrate than to give what at times you may not have? Hope and faith were to Mother Teresa what loaves and fishes were to Jesus. She just kept giving both, and they miraculously kept coming.

Is this not what truly makes one a saint? Is a saint one who is perfect, flawless, faith-filled, and unhesitant? Or could a saint be a hungry soul who feeds not just her own doubting spirit but the spirit of millions of others worldwide, inspired by her example? Mother Teresa is no longer that tiny fragile woman surrounded by unimaginable poverty. In death, she stands tall, surrounded by unimaginable riches. Her journey teaches us that faith and fear can walk together.

Mother Teresa reached out to the poorest of the poor. Her faith inspired her to do so, but so, too, did her knowledge of what it felt like to go to bed hungry and lonely in a world at war. She kept on giving when she had little to give. Her struggles made her human. Her actions may very well make her a saint. Her life shines not because she stood on the extremes but because she rejected them, choosing instead to serve from the center at the very nexus of the cross.

14.

RECONCILING FAITH
WITH ACTION

BUNKER HILL, VALLEY FORGE, HARPER'S FERRY, Gettysburg, Selma—these sites call to mind an evolving American ideal forged in a crucible of intense spiritual heat. They speak of an ideal strong enough to meet present challenges but supple enough to meet the challenges of the future. They speak to our very identity as a people. Out of the womb of taxation without representation, this nation emerged as a global beacon of self-rule and democracy. From the steamy summer corridors of pre–air-conditioned Philadelphia flowed the documents that affirmed life, ignited liberty, and compelled us to pursue happiness.

Throughout the course of American history, this great nation successfully overcame incredible obstacles not just by might or power or economic resilience, but by the ability to reshape itself, at the right moment, always better than before. Unlike many nations convulsed by revolution—France comes to mind—our nation has adapted to the future without forgetting the past. In fact, our greatest transitions have come in our attempt to honor the past, to fulfill our destiny as a nation, to pay down our debt to the Creator who endowed us with unalienable rights.

This is something not everyone understands. In the Declaration of Independence we established what we hoped to be as a nation. In the Constitution, drafted about a dozen years later, we set down the guidelines as to how we expected to get there. At the time, everyone understood changes would have to be made down the road for us to become what the Preamble to the Constitution described as "a more perfect union."

From the beginning, the greatest stumbling block both to perfection and to unity was slavery. The nature of the institution warred with the essential "created equal" phrasing of the Declaration. Yet, the founders from the Northern states knew that without the cooperation of their Southern brethren there would be no Declaration, no Constitution, no United States. Disunited, we would likely dissolve into the kind of squabbling factionalism seen in the Balkans. Historically, chronic disunity left those nations so vulnerable that their people were easy prey for the North African warlords. The very word *slave* derives from *Slav*. These poor people lent their name to that sorry institution.

Given the reality on the ground, our nation was born out of compromise. Ironically, it was the anti-slavery advocates in the North who insisted that slaves count as no more than three-fifths of a person. The pro-slavery South wanted them to count as a whole person to increase the South's congressional representation and its subsequent power to expand the slavery franchise.

This issue could not be left unresolved forever. More than six hundred thousand Americans died in slavery's bloody resolution. Never before had a nation gone to war to end slavery. Yet, as we know, even that sacrifice did not solve the problem completely.

When he ascended onto the main stage with the mission to resolve unresolved wrongs, Martin Luther King Jr. did what many transformative Americans in the past had done. King asked America not to discard its highest laws, but to honor them. What follows comes from his 1963 "I Have A Dream" speech:

> In a sense we have come to our nation's capital to cash a check. When the architects of our republic wrote the magnificent words of the Constitution and the Declaration of Independence, they were signing a promissory note to which every American was to fall heir. This note was a promise that all men, yes, black men as well as white men, would be guaranteed the unalienable rights of life, liberty, and the pursuit of happiness.

It was no accident that King was a Baptist minister, representing the Southern Christian Leadership Conference. It was more like a prophecy fulfilled. The impetus to end slavery came entirely from committed Christians, most of them evangelical. Their spiritual heirs continue to fight against slavery in those parts of the world where it persists.

Those among us who condemn America for its historical slavery would do well to study the history of one Francis Bok. Bok grew up in a large Catholic family in a Dinka village in the south of Sudan. As a seven-year-old in 1986, Bok was taken captive by an Islamic militia and sold into slavery. It would take him ten years to escape. With the help of a brave and kindly Muslim, Bok made his way to Cairo where he sought refuge in a Catholic church. From there, the Lutheran Social Services and the United Methodists arranged for his passage to the United States. After a few years getting settled, the deeply Christian Bok began his real life's work as a modern-day abolitionist. In 2002, he met with President George W. Bush in the White House, becoming the first former slave to meet an American president since the nineteenth century.[1]

America was not at all unique in its uneasy tolerance of slavery. It was entirely unique, however, in the sacrifice it made in blood and treasure to end it. Those today who are convinced that they would not have tolerated slavery under any circumstances need to ask themselves what they have done to end legal abortion, the unholy practice that has claimed fifty million innocent lives since Roe v. Wade in 1973. As evil as slavery was, slaveholders had an economic interest in keeping slaves alive and even healthy. Abortionists have the reverse charge. Ending abortion is the major civil rights challenge of the day. It is one more hurdle to overcome on our journey to become "a more perfect union."

Voting Vertical

We are blessed to live in a nation in which Peter's injunction to respect civil authority presents few moral challenges:

> Submit yourselves for the Lord's sake to every human authority: whether to the emperor, as the supreme authority, or to governors, who are sent by him to punish those who do wrong and to commend those who do right. For it is God's will that by doing good you should silence the ignorant talk of foolish people. Live as free people, but do not use your freedom as a cover-up for evil; live as God's slaves. Show proper respect to everyone, love the family of believers, fear God, honor the emperor. (1 Peter 2:13–17)

Obviously, not all the laws we live under are just. The Supreme Court's decision to make abortion a constitutional right, for instance, violated not only God's law but the very spirit of the Constitution. And yet even Roe v. Wade is within our power as citizens to overturn nonviolently through the political process. We can vote for a president who will appoint judges who see Roe v. Wade for the judicial overreach it is. Or we can go through the more difficult but perhaps more appropriate steps entailed in a constitutional amendment.

What we need to do, though, every time we enter a voting booth, is to assess in advance how we expect to align our vote with God's will. This is not always easy. In fact, it is rarely easy. We will sometimes find competing candidates, each of whom seems to represent different elements of God's plan. On other occasions, we will have to choose between a good short-term candidate and a better long-term party.

In every case, we have to beware of political strategists who exploit our Christianity to get our vote. Interest groups on a wide range of issues that have almost nothing to do with faith will appeal to the cross. In some cases, they will argue that their pet cause—say, saving the whale—is as demanding of the Christian vote as, say, saving an unborn baby. They may even quote Scripture in the process. They may bundle a package of marginal causes and tell you that, together, they outweigh a core conviction of a Bible-believing Christian.

In some cases, we may encounter laws so unjust and so resistant to political change that we may have to contemplate civil disobedience. Martin Luther King Jr. faced this dilemma on several occasions. Here is how he resolved it in his famous "Letter from the Birmingham Jail": "One who breaks an unjust law that conscience tells him is unjust, and who willingly accepts the penalty of imprisonment in order to arouse the conscience of the community over its injustice, is in reality expressing the highest respect for law."[2]

What King did was to appeal to the larger nation by resisting local laws that warred with the spirit of the nation's founding. Although breaking the law, he stayed within the system by acting nonviolently and by appealing to the nation's conscience.

I would not be surprised, in fact, if the Third Great Awakening were inspired by an act of civil disobedience, perhaps a mass act of civil disobedience. I suspect, too, that this transformative act, this kingdom culture Concord Bridge, will take its name from the one church that had the will to resist when resistance was all that was left for a Christian to do.

SANCTIFICATION AND SERVICE

The umbrella organization for "volunteering" in America is called the Corporation for National and Community Service (CNCS). When I Googled the CNCS, the first three headings to appear were "New Founding Opportunities," "eGrants," and "Employment."[3] This gives you some sense of what service work in a billion-dollar-plus government organization is all about. I am sure there are good people working there, but I am also sure there are many people in power at CNCS whose primary job is to advance the political fortunes of the person who appointed them.

We can be pretty confident that Jesus did not have CNCS in mind when he said, as recorded in Matthew 25:34–36, the following words of wisdom:

Come, you who are blessed by my Father; take your inheritance, the kingdom prepared for you since the creation of the world. For I was hungry and you gave me something to eat, I was thirsty and you gave me something to drink, I was a stranger and you invited me in, I needed clothes and you clothed me, I was sick and you looked after me, I was in prison and you came to visit me.

The sanctified do not read the benefits page on an organization's website before deciding whether to feed the hungry or welcome the stranger. When these instincts are politicized, they deprive the giver of the opportunity to do good for its own sake and the recipient the opportunity to appreciate the good that has been done.

In 2011, for instance, a Michigan woman won a million-dollar state lottery and decided to take her winnings as a $700,000 cash payment. What she did not do is report her winnings to the state Department of Human Services. In fact, she continued to receive and use food stamps, paid for by the taxpayers of Michigan, the great majority of whom had less money than she did.[4] Although this is an extreme example, the design of the welfare systems makes cheaters out of a lot of people. Once dependent on the state, recipients are easily exploited by politicians who vie to sway their votes by promising them more of other people's money.

When stories like that of the Michigan lottery winner make the news, they deaden the charitable impulse of even generous people and make cynics out of the good-spirited. Our mission as kingdom culture Christians is to transcend that cynicism. When we see a need we should fill it, either personally or through an organized response by our church community. This is who we are as a people, who we have to be.

There is something else to consider: Christian charity is situated fully at the nexus of the cross. In both the New Testament and the Old, one gave alms as much to please God as to help the poor. The English word *creditor*, for instance, derives from the Latin *credere*—"to believe." In a very real sense, to give to the poor is to testify to one's belief in God. As Jesus told the rich young man in Matthew 19:21, "If you want to be perfect, go, sell your possessions and give to the poor, and you will have treasure in heaven. Then come, follow me." The payoff was to be expected not on earth, but in heaven. This is something that no state bureaucracy can understand.

To be fair, the National Christian Foundation, the largest Christian grant-making foundation in the world, also deals with the details of grant writing and tax deductions, but the spirit that motivates the giving is radically different and so are the results. "I will pour out my Spirit on all people," reads Joel 2:28. "Your sons and daughters will prophesy, your old men will dream dreams, your young men will see visions."[5] Since 1982 the Foundation has made more than $3 billion in grants to thousands of churches, ministries, and nonprofits.

Not a single one of those dollars was coerced. Not a single would-be donor fled the country or filed a false return to avoid having to give. Not a single recipient thought it his or her "right" to receive a gift. No grouping of recipients formed a collective to demand more. And so few of those dollars were wasted or squandered or extorted that it would not even pay to track them. This is the way the Lamb's Agenda works. The best government cannot match its efficiency or even dream of capturing its spirit.

15.

BEHOLD THE LAMB

OUR VERTICAL RELATIONSHIP CARRIES HORIZONTAL consequences, and our horizontal relationships carry vertical consequences. Relationships are a matter of choice. Life is about choices. The choices we make today will determine the lives we live tomorrow. We have the choice to believe or not believe, to follow a dream or succumb to a nightmare, to lift our heads or walk in sorrow, to stay in the desert or march toward the promised land. We have a choice to live by faith or walk by sight, to look back or push forward, to stay silent because of sin or shout for joy because of grace. We have a choice today, a choice between living in the valley or ruling from the mountaintop.

This is the choice that Abraham made when he stood determined to climb with his sacrifice, hoping for the lamb:

Abraham took the wood for the burnt offering and placed it
on his son Isaac, and he himself carried the fire and the knife.

As the two of them went on together, Isaac spoke up and said to his father Abraham, "Father?"

"Yes, my son?" Abraham replied.

"The fire and wood are here," Isaac said, "but where is the lamb for the burnt offering?" (Genesis 22:6–7)

WHAT WE CARRY TODAY WILL BE OUR BED FOR TOMORROW

Isaac carried the wood to the very place to which he would be bound in a short while. We should ask ourselves, what are we carrying? The fact is that what we carry up will determine what we bring down. What we carry today will be our bed tomorrow. If we carry bitterness, we will lie on bitterness. If we carry hatred, we will be bound to hatred. If we carry envy, we will lie on envy. But if we carry joy, if we carry peace, if we carry love, if we carry righteousness, we will rest on joy, peace, love, and righteousness in the Holy Ghost. In essence, we will rest in the bounty of the kingdom of God.

HOLD ON TO THE FIRE

Notice how Abraham gave Isaac the wood, but who carried the fire? Abraham carried the fire. Hold on to the fire! You see, the fire must always be in our hands. Everyone can carry the wood, everyone can carry the goods, but if we have the fire, all things are possible.

When Gideon's army fought the Midianites, the fire was

in his army's hands. When Elijah instructed them to put more water on the wood, he called out for the fire.

John the Baptist said, "I baptize you with water, but one who is more powerful than I will come. The straps of whose sandals I am not worthy to untie. He will baptize you with the Holy Spirit and fire" (Luke 3:16).

Fire is the fuel for justice; fire is the hunger for righteousness. Who will climb and conquer? Those who don't let go of the fire! God is looking for a man or a woman who still holds on to the fire—the desire to do what's right even in the midst of criticism, persecution, and possibly imprisonment or death.

WHERE IS THE LAMB?

Isaac then asked the $100 million question, "I see the fire, I see the wood, but *where is the Lamb?*" Sometimes, we find ourselves asking the same question: God, I prayed. I fasted. I confessed, but where is the answer? And just like with Abraham, the answer is that God will provide.

Where is the lamb? For two thousand years humanity asked the same question and then the answer came in John 1:29, "Behold! The Lamb of God who takes away the sin of the world!" (NKJV). Jesus is the Lamb.

Once again, humanity cries out, "Where is the Lamb?" From all strata of society, men and women, children and elders, cry out for the Lamb. Let us rise up and respond with the answer of John the Baptist, "Behold! the Lamb of God."

Let this generation shake off the shackles of complacency and mediocrity while declaring, "Behold the Lamb! Behold the

Lamb who brings forth righteousness and justice. Behold the Lamb who activates sanctification and service. Behold the Lamb who reconciles the message with the march, Billy Graham with Dr. King, holiness with humility, orthodoxy with orthopraxy, *imago Dei* with *habitus Christus*, truth with love."

The apostle John saw the Lamb seated on the throne. Not only did the Father provide the Lamb, but he also seated the Lamb on the throne, which means the Lamb rules and governs. As long as the Lamb is on the throne, there is hope.

On a trip to Israel, I visited an olive tree farm. The director of the farm and surrounding campground pointed to an olive tree and asked me to guess the age of the tree. I responded, "One or two hundred years old." She replied, "That tree is somewhere between fifteen hundred and two thousand years old."

I asked, "How can a tree can survive that long?" She quickly replied, "That tree has experienced fires and droughts, and it still stands. Simply, the roots are embedded within the rock. As long as the rock does not move, that tree will live."

Christ is our rock. As long as our rock, the Lamb, is on the throne, there is hope for our nation, hope for our children, hope for our faith, and hope for humanity. As long as the Lamb is on the throne, faith, hope, and charity will live.

Revelation 5:5 tells us that it is the Lamb who is capable of opening what others cannot open.

And Revelation 5:9 tells us that it is the Lamb who produces a new song.

In Revelation 12:11 we learn of the survivors in their battle against Satan, who "triumphed over him by the blood of the Lamb and by the word of their testimony; they did not love their lives so much as to shrink from death."

The Lamb's Agenda opens the book and reveals truth. The

Lamb's agenda produces a new song, the song of the redeemed. The Lamb's agenda enables us to overcome. For we cannot dance in the promised land until we learn to sing in the desert.

Therefore, let us press forward with the Agenda of the Lamb. Let us speak to the barrio and Beverly Hills, to those on Wall Street and Main Street, to all in this generation tired of partisan politics, tired of archaic nomenclature, tired of discord and strife, but hungry for righteousness and justice.

To you I say, let us stand up and declare, "Behold! The Lamb of God who takes away the sin of all mankind."

By doing so, by reconciling Billy Graham's righteousness message with Martin Luther King's justice march we will one day sing:

"TO HIM WHO SITS ON THE THRONE AND TO THE LAMB BE PRAISE AND HONOR AND GLORY AND POWER, FOR EVER AND EVER!" (REVELATIONS 5:13)

ACKNOWLEDGMENTS

I WANT TO ACKNOWLEDGE THE TWO INDIVIDUALS who inspired me to reconcile conviction with compassion, truth with love, and righteousness with justice: Billy Graham and Dr. Martin Luther King Jr.

In addition, Bill Dallas, Jay Mitchell, Thomas Nelson team and, of course, Jack Cashill. Thank you all for believing.

Finally, to my wife, children, family, and church community: your prayers pushed me through and here we stand committed to advancing the Lamb's Agenda.

NOTES

Introduction: The Third Great Awakening

1. Charles Dickens, *A Tale of Two Cities* (New York: Scribners and Sons, 1867), 1.
2. Tacitus, *Annals*, XV, trans. by Alfred John Church and William Jackson Brodribb, *The Internet Classics Archive*.
3. Maureen Cleave, "How Does A Beatle Live?" *London Evening Standard*, March 4, 1966.

Chapter 1: A Cross Movement, Vertical and Horizontal

1. For a complete retelling of this story, see Eric Metaxsas, *Bonhoeffer: Pastor, Martyr, Prophet, Spy* (Nashville: Thomas Nelson, 2010).
2. Although there are different versions of this text, this is the exact text of what Martin Niemöller said in his address to the US Congress, and which appears in the Congressional Record, October 14, 1968, page 31636.
3. "Chinese authorities expel Shouwang Church member from Beijing," *Christianity Today*, June 30, 2011.
4. "In Opposing the Right to Same-Sex Marriage, Catholic Leadership Opposes Laity and Wider Public," *Rainbow Sash Movement*, February 9, 2012.

5. As cited in Greg Gordon, "Revival At Any Cost!" Gospel.com.

6. Kansas Evolution Hearings, Part 6, *The TalkOrigins Archive*.

7. William Provine, *Academe*, January/February 1987, 51–52.

8. Ibid.

9. Reinhard Hutter, "Flight from Sadness," delivered as a sermon at the First Congregation Church in Harwich, Massachusetts, April 1, 2012.

10. Henry David Thoreau, *Walden, or Life in the Woods* (Forgotten Books, forgottenbooks.org, 2008), 228.

11. Linda Ronstadt, "Different Drum," written and composed by Michael Nesmith before he joined the Monkees, 1967.

12. Jimi Hendrix, "If 6 was 9," recorded by the Jimi Hendrix Experience, 1967.

13. "My Way," written by Paul Anka and recorded by Frank Sinatra, 1968.

14. John Lennon, interviewed by Jonathan Colt on December 5, 1980, appeared in *Rolling Stone*, January 22, 1981.

15. Ibid.

16. As quoted in "Aftershock," Angelfire.com.

17. Edward Mote, public domain, 1834.

Chapter 2: Prophetic vs. Pathetic Movements

1. Exodus 9:1.

2. Joshua 24:15 (NKJV).

3. 1 Samuel 17:45.

4. Daniel 3:19–25.

5. Thomas Jefferson, *Declaration of Independence*, July 2, 1776.

6. Abraham Lincoln, Second Inaugural Address, March 4, 1865.

7. Martin Luther King Jr., "I Have a Dream" speech, August 28, 1963.

8. Ronald Reagan, National Prayer Breakfast speech, January 31, 1985.

9. Isaiah 6:3.

10. *Declaration of Independence*, July 2, 1776.

11. Tape Number Q 134, Jonestown Audiotape Primary Project, transcript prepared by Fielding M. McGehee, III, The Jonestown Institute.

12. Antonio Gramsci, selections from cultural writings (London: Lawrence & Wishart, 1985), 41.

13. George Whitefield, "The Lord Our Righteousness" sermon, http://www.anglicanlibrary.org/whitefield/sermons/14.htm.

14. John Bartlett, *Barlett's Familiar Quotations*, 16th Edition, John Wesley (Little, Brown, & Co., 1992), 309.

15. John Wesley, *The Means of Grace, A Sermon on Malachi iii.7*, Gale ECCO, Print Editions (June 24, 2010).

16. William Lloyd Garrison, "On the Death of John Brown," Great Speeches Collection, The History Place.

17. Scott Clement, "The Tea Party, Religion and Social Issues," *Pew Research Center Publications*, February 23, 2011.

18. David Sessions, "The Christian Right in Disguise?" *The Daily Beast*, August 18, 2011.

19. Jon Brand, "Tea party: Libertarian revolt or religious right in disguise?" *Christian Science Monitor*, April 21, 2011.

20. Tim Koelkebeck, "Is the Religious Right Taking Over the Tea Party?" *Huffington Post*, October 27, 2010.

21. "Anti-Semitic Protester at Occupy Wall Street—LA," YouTube.com, October 14, 2011.

22. Joseph Berger, "Cries of Anti-Semitism, but Not at Zuccotti Park," *New York Times*, October 21, 2011.

23. Cindy Wooden, "Vatican officials see agreement in church teaching, Occupy Wall Street," *The Catholic Register*, October 24, 2011.

24. Lisa Miller, "Jesus at Occupy Wall Street: 'I feel like I've been here before,' " *Washington Post*, October 20, 2011.

Chapter 3: Not The Donkey, Not the Elephant, but the Lamb

1. Myles Collier, "Gallup Poll Church Attendance: Republicans Attend More Services Than Democrats," *Christian Post*, November 9, 2011.

2. Kevin Merida and Helen Dewar, "In Boom of Phone and Fax Activism, Citizens Give Government an Earful," *The Washington Post* (February 1, 1993): A1.

3. *Religulous*, "Memorable Quotes," imdb.com.

4. Ibid.

5. Katherine Phan, "Hollywood Celebrities Mock Christians in Anti-Prop. 8 Video," *Christian Post*, December 8, 2008.

6. John Lennon, "Imagine," 1971. See complete lyrics at www.oldielyrics.com/lyrics/john_lennon/imagine.html.

7. Abraham Lincoln, "Second Inaugural Address," March 4, 1865, www.bartleby.com.

8. "America's Godly Heritage," *Jeremiah Project*.

9. Jesse Jackson, reprinted as "How we respect life is the overriding moral issue," *Right to Life News*, January 1977.

10. Ibid.

11. Ted Kennedy, letter to Catholic League member Tom Dennelly, 1971, "Ted Kennedy, Abortion Advocate and Health Reform Mastermind, Dead at 77," *LifeSiteNews.com*, August 26, 2009.

12. Arthur C. Brooks, *Who Really Cares: America's Charity Divide: Who Gives, Who Doesn't, And Why It Really Matters* (New York: Basic Books, 2006).

13. Ibid., 22.

Chapter 4: Righteousness and Justice

1. C. S. Lewis, *God in the Dock: Essays on Theology and Ethics*.

2. Jack Cashill: *Hoodwinked: How Intellectual Hucksters Have Hijacked American Culture* (Nashville: Thomas Nelson, 2005), 31.

3. Michelle Brock, "Meet An Abolitionist: William Wilberforce," *Hope For The Sold*, April 1, 2011.

4. Susan Verstraete, "William Wilberforce and the Great Change," bulletininserts.org.

5. Rusty Wright, "William Wilberforce and Abolishing the Slave Trade," probe.org.

6. Kevin Belmonte, *William Wilberforce: A Hero for Humanity* (Grand Rapids: Zondervan, 2007), 90.

7. *The Big Book*, anonpress.org, 13.

8. Ibid., 14.

9. Ibid.

10. Martin Luther King, Jr., "Where Do We Go From Here?" 1967, as published in *Where Do We Go from Here: Chaos or Community?* (Boston: Beacon Press, 2010), 62.

11. Martin Luther King, Jr., "Address to the first Montgomery Improvement Association Mass Meeting," December 5, 1955.

12. "Charles W. Colson," prisonfellowship.org.

13. David Kinnaman and Gabe Lyons, *unChristian: What a New Generation Really Thinks about Christianity . . . and Why It Matters*, (Baker Books, 2007), 174.

14. "An Interview With Charles Colson," Assemblies of God, ag.org.

15. Jack Cashill, *What's the Matter With California* (New York: Simon & Schuster, 2007), 240.

16. Joe Matthews, "Labor Is Backing Abortion Rights," *Los Angeles Times,* August 7, 2006.

17. Steve Macias, "Sierra College Dishonors Chávez Legacy with Pro-Abortion Forum," studentsforlife.org, March 16, 2012.

Chapter 5: Reconciling Billy Graham with Martin Luther King Jr.

1. Author's recollection.

2. "Why 'Christianity Today'?" *Christianity Today,* October 15, 1956.

3. Laura Hillenbrand, *Unbroken: a World War II story of survival, resilience, and redemption* (New York; Random House, 2010), 370.

4. Ibid., 376.

5. Gary Krist, "Laura Hillenbrand's 'Unbroken,' " *Washington Post,* November 12, 2010.

6. Alexander J. Sheffrin, "Alveda King Calls Abortion 'Racist.'" *Christian Post,* April 15, 2008.

7. Ira F. Stanphill, © 1946 New Spring (Admin. by Universal Music Publishing MGB Australia Pty)

Chapter 6: Reconciling John 3:16 with Matthew 25

1. Kevin Dolak, "Bill Maher Courts Controversy Over Tim Tebow Tweet," *ABC News,* December 28, 2011.

2. "Locker Room," *SNL Transcripts,* December 17, 2011.

3. Kate Alexander, "On Easter Sunday, Tebow Is a Headliner," *New York Times,* April 8, 2012.

4. Joe Tacopino, "Women's Groups Protest Tim Tebow's Pro-life Super Bowl Ad for Focus on the Family," *New York Daily News,* January 26, 2010.

5. Tim Tebow "'Focus on the Family' Super Bowl Commercial Video," *Bookroom Reviews,* February 7, 2010.

6. Tim Tebow, *Through My Eyes: A Quarterback's Journey:* (New York: HarperCollins, 2011), 57.

7. Ibid., 29.
8. All quotes that follow from "Interview with Hal Donaldson,"
   AGTV, May 26, 2010.

Chapter 7: A Kingdom Culture Movement

1. Luis Lugo, "Here Come 'Los Evangélicos'!" *PewResearchCenter Publications*, June 6, 2007.
2. Samuel Roderiquez, "Mercy Rising—A Call to Love the Immigrant," *Enrichment Journal*.
3. Ibid.
4. Ibid.
5. Ibid.
6. Ibid.
7. Ibid.
8. Ibid.
9. Ibid.
10. Ibid.
11. "Analysis of California Proposition 8 Exit Poll Data," www.madpickles.org.
12. "The Manhattan Declaration," manhattandeclaration.org.

Chapter 8: An HD or Analog Movement

1. "Religion Among the Millennials," *The Pew Forum on Religion & Public Life*, February 17, 2010.
2. Nancy Dillon, "Whitney Houston told friends her end was near," *New York Daily News*, February 15, 2012.
3. "Barton W. Stone on the Perfect Creed," *The Fellowship Room*, October 21, 2010.

Chapter 9: John the Baptist Leadership

1. "Go Down Moses" is an American Negro spiritual of uncertain vintage. It describes events in Exodus 7:16.

Chapter 10: Reconciling the Vertical Lamb with the Horizontal Lion

1. Dereck Joubert, *The Last Lions*, 2011, as remembered by the author.
2. Flannery O'Connor, *Wiseblood* (New York: Farrar, Strauss and Giroux, 1990), 101.

3. Billy Graham, "A Time for Moral Courage," *Reader's Digest*, July 1964.

4. "The Manhattan Declaration," manhattandeclaration.org.

5. S. E. Cupp, *Losing Our Religion: The Liberal Media's Attack on Christianity* (New York: Simon & Schuster, 2010), 53–54.

6. Barack Obama, Saddleback Presidential Candidates Forum, August 17, 2008.

7. Barack Obama, *The Audacity of Hope: Thoughts on Reclaiming the American Dream* (New York: Random House, 2006), 222.

8. Carrie Prejean, *Still Standing: The Untold Story of My Fight Against Gossip, Hate, and Political Attacks* (Washington: Regnery, 2009), 221.

9. "The Manhattan Declaration," manhattandeclaration.org.

10. Matthew Cortina, "Faith Group Protests Southern Poverty Law Center Over 'Hate Group' Label," *Christian Post*, January 17, 2012.

11. Todd Starnes, "Proposed Law Would Force Churches to Host Gay Weddings," *FOX News*, April 23, 2012.

12. Ibid.

13. "Dan Savage discusses The Holy Bible at a Seattle High School Journalism convention," YouTube, youtube.com/watch?v=uzrxhzHxBlU.

14. "Circular by various Protestant ministers on behalf of the activities of the New England Emigrant Aid Company," *Territorial Kansas Online*, 1854-1961.

15. Eli Thayer, "The Suicide of Slavery," delivered in the House of Representatives, March 25, 1858.

16. "Phill Kline at the Eagle Forum," YouTube.com.

17. For a complete discussion, see, Jack Cashill, "The Man Behind The Curtain," KFL.org.

Chapter 11: Reconciling Plymouth Rock with Jamestown

1. George Washington, letter, March 11, 1792.

2. See usconstitution.net/mayflower.html for complete document.

3. Caleb Johnson ed., *William Bradford: Of Plymouth Plantation* (Bloomington, IN: Xlibris, 2006), 171.

4. Religiousfreedom.lib.virginia.edu/sacred/charity.html for complete document.

5. "God Bless America" is controlled by Irving Berlin Music, a

division of Williamson Music. It is not in the public domain. Licensing proceeds benefit the Boy Scouts of America.

6. The Marseillaise is in the public domain in the United States.
7. See constitution.org/fr/fr_drm.htm for complete text.
8. John O'Sullivan, "Annexation," *Democratic Review,* July-August, 1845.
9. Caleb Johnson, 257.
10. Jeremiah Evarts, "A Brief View," *New York Observer,* December 16, 1829.
11. Thomas Jefferson, *Notes on the State of Virginia,* 1785, Chapter 18, American Studies at the University of Virginia, xroads.virginia.edu.
12. Harriet Beecher Stowe, thinkexist.com.
13. Ronald Reagan, Official Announcement of Candidacy for President, November 13, 1979.
14. John Winthrop, "A Model of Christian Charity."
15. "U.S. Supreme Court Upholds Ministerial Exemption," HR.BLR.com, January 12, 2012.
16. George Washington, letter, March 11, 1792.

Chapter 12: Reconciling *Imago Dei* with *Habitus Christus*

1. Kyle Smith, "Wait A Minute—Why Should I Hate Bernie Madoff?" Forbes.com, February 9, 2011.

Chapter 13: The Nexus of the Cross

1. "Biography: Mother Teresa of Calcutta (1910-1997)," *Vatican News Service.*

Chapter 14: Reconciling Faith with Action

1. "About Francis Bok," The Francis Bok Foundation.
2. Martin Luther King, "Letter from the Birmingham Jail," April 16, 1963.
3. Corporation for National and Community Service, nationalservice.gov.
4. Jeff Black, "Michigan lottery winner charged with welfare fraud," msnbc.com, April 17, 2012.
5. National Christian Foundation, nationalchristian.com.

Scripture Index

INDEX

ABOUT THE AUTHOR

REV. SAMUEL RODRIGUEZ IS PRESIDENT OF THE National Hispanic Christian Leadership Conference, America's largest Hispanic Christian organization. Named by CNN as "The leader of the Hispanic Evangelical Movement" and by the *San Francisco Chronicle* as one of America's new evangelical leaders, Rodriguez is also the recipient of the Martin Luther King Jr. Award presented by the Congress on Racial Equality. A featured speaker in White House and congressional meetings, he has been featured, profiled, and quoted by such media outlets as the *New York Times*, *Christianity Today*, *Washington Post*, *Wall Street Journal*, *Newsweek*, Univision, Fox News, *Time*, and *Ministries Today*. Rodriguez is also the Senior Pastor of New Season Christian Worship Center in Sacramento, California.